DO THE WORK ONCE, GET PAID FOREVER

Do the Work **Once,**
Get Paid **Forever**

HOW SMART PEOPLE
INVEST IN REAL ESTATE

JOHN BOGDASARIAN

LIONCREST
PUBLISHING

DO THE WORK ONCE, GET PAID FOREVER

How Smart People Invest in Real Estate

ISBN   978-1-5445-0454-4 *Paperback*
       978-1-5445-0453-7 *Ebook*

Contents

Introduction

Full disclosure: I'm not a writer. English was never my strongest subject in school. Actually, other than math, I don't think I had many strong subjects in school—maybe public speaking.

I've written out my words in conversational tone on the following pages, and I hope you will find the information useful and informative. My ultimate goal is to help get the world's real wealth distributed among as many people as possible without using law, taxes, or incentives. I want people to KNOW what real wealth is AND to earn it for themselves.

I also want people to teach it to the next generation. What is real wealth? For me, it's owning great real estate. There are other ways to create wealth; however, I don't personally know anyone truly wealthy who doesn't own some substantial real estate as part of their holdings.

This book is written for professionals and business owners who have limited time and energy to nitpick the details of real estate investment deals. It's for people who have money to invest in real estate but need a good steward for that money—somebody who will take care of it. I hope a few younger deal sponsors out there find it useful as well.

I sincerely hope that you find this information useful and that you will share it with others as well. This project took a lot longer (and was WAY more difficult) than anticipated. I have the utmost respect for REAL writers, and I wouldn't dare call this a real book. Having the combination of my skillset AND being able to write doesn't really seem highly probable, because if someone spent their entire life getting the real estate experience that I have, then they'd have no time to practice and learn how to write properly.

Some people say that you shouldn't put a crappy book out there. That's okay; almost all my teachers thought I was a major distraction and wouldn't amount to much. Fortunately, I had amazing parents who supported me (especially you, Mom) no matter what my report cards looked like. I didn't listen to the people who told me I wouldn't amount to much. I didn't listen to all the people who told me I should study hard and get a "good" job. I never listen to bankers who turn down financing for my projects. And I don't see the point in listening to people who tell me not to put out a book.

Don't let people rob you of all the things you are capable of doing, all the help you are capable of providing, and the wealth you are capable of building. There's way more to this than the money—you will see what I mean.

I would like to thank everyone I've ever come in contact with because I've learned from you all. From my first memories around age four or five all the way to today (age forty-nine right now), I have been blessed to be able to observe and learn from amazing people. While my goals have changed over time, every single one of them has been met (except the whole movie star thing), and there's plenty of track left (even though it has a lot less to do with money now).

I learn by setting clear goals and then working to achieve them. Many people will cast doubt on you and your goals, and I like to say, "There's no good argument for not trying."

I tried to write this book, I wrote it, and I learned more from doing it than I would have from not doing it. I hope you find it useful and worthwhile. Cheers! And thanks for giving it a go...

CHAPTER ONE

Why Invest in Real Estate

I assume that if you've picked up this book, you're interested in real estate already, or you're interested in the real estate space in general, right? If you're like me, you enjoy reading books about the positives of this industry, and there are many. In fact, if you're reading this, you're ahead of where I was when I first started. I learned a lot of things the hard way, by trial and error, and I later learned (as I became successful) that there is a wealth of knowledge out there. In this book, you'll reap the rewards of my own hard-won knowledge, and I'll also point you to other fantastic resources.

REAL ESTATE INVESTING ISN'T SEXY

Maybe it is. This all depends on your view of sexy. If your mission in life is to gain stature and wealth, you can do it through real estate; however, real estate investing can be boring and slow-moving. The best deals *should* be boring. The sexier they are, the worse they tend to be—usually.

Real estate tends to be stable and predictable. Everything moves VERY slowly. If you're paying attention, you can and should always be one step ahead of things. You don't need to be right on top of the latest news and information because it moves slowly. You have months to try to figure things out. When we talk about real estate being bricks and mortar, literally, you're buying something tangible. You can touch it and feel it.

The stock market provides intangible financial products—conjured items, if you will. You may have a claim on a company's earnings if you're a partial owner, but you're such a small piece that you have no say in what happens. If you invested in Ford when it initially went public, at times you'd be very wealthy (on paper) and at other times broke, and then you'd be rich again. If you hold a stock long enough, eventually you will lose your money because every company ultimately goes out of business. No company lasts forever. That's the reality of companies. Think about it: how many times have you driven by a restaurant you knew, only to discover that it had closed or that all of a sudden, there was another restaurant in its place? It happens all the time. Businesses come and go. But real estate lasts forever in the sense that a location is not going to go out of business. Whoever owns the property of that restaurant (or retail space, or office building) is still getting the rent check. Someone will be putting a business there, and the only sure way to make money is to own the space, not the business. The businesses that rent from us come and go. We want them to be successful, of course, but because we're in real estate, we never go out of business as long as we buy solid locations.

Whatever real estate you own—whether it's a home, an office, a warehouse, or a factory—it provides value. It provides a space where someone can do something that creates value for others. It seems so simple to me, and it should to you. At minimum, real estate investments should represent at least 20 percent of your portfolio—they represent 80 percent of mine. The trick is finding the right people to invest with, and that's what this book is about.

DIVERSIFICATION IS IMPORTANT

Even though I invest heavily in real estate, I understand that diversification is important to financial success. It leads to greater returns and better sleep at night, knowing all of your money isn't tied up in one thing. For most people, anyway.

My rule of thumb is to divide investment funds into three to five different baskets. There are many ways to accomplish this. For example, you could choose to put 20 percent into real estate and the remaining 80 percent in other investment avenues such as stocks or bonds.

Another option, and obviously my preferred one, is to put the majority of investment funds into real estate but diversify within that arena. Own buildings in different geographic regions, or diversify by investing in different building types. For example, I own industrial buildings, apartment complexes, multi-tenant office buildings, and residential units. I invest in development projects as well. We build condominium buildings and sell out the units, we build hotels and keep them for cash flow or sell them to REITs, and we take raw land and develop it into buildable lots so people have a place to live.

Most importantly, if you follow this book and choose to work with a real estate partner, do not put more than 20 percent of your money with one person. Find five different deal sponsors that do real estate really well, and allocate 20 percent of your funds to each of them.

NOTE: Beware of financial advisors and have an understanding of how they are compensated. The financial advisory industry is known for pushing their clients into investments that make the advisors money. Or, at the very least, they are highly motivated to keep your money under their umbrella so they can get paid on it. Almost no investment advisors are set up to make any money by seeking out real estate investment deals like the ones we will talk about here. We are not regulated by the SEC, and therefore we don't pay brokers to put people in our deals. In fact, most stockbrokers are not legally allowed to recommend investments like ours. More on this later.

I want you to understand how financial advisors are compensated and how that affects where they invest your money. You're smart, and I know you'll keep track of your investments. Once you've diversified for a while, you may consider consolidating some investments based on your returns and preferred growth strategy.

THE DOWNSIDE OF REAL ESTATE

The downside of real estate investing is...well, it doesn't really have one—if done correctly. The downside is getting into the wrong real estate investments with the wrong people. If it's done the right way, the risk is very, very low. You're unlikely to lose all of your capital in real estate, as long as you're doing it the right way: not taking on too much leverage or using rosy projections. Yes, there are a lot of mistakes that can be made, and yes, there are bad people who want to make big fees at your expense. That's what this book is going to help you avoid.

A quick example: My investment group is currently building a hotel in Denver. If we open the hotel and don't hit our initial projections, it's okay. Perhaps there's a blip in the market, or occupancy rates go down, or we just don't generate the income we expected. It doesn't matter in the long run because the building is still there, the product is still there, and things will eventually go back up. Real estate investment requires patience and dedication. As room rates increase, as you improve operations, as you get more people to review it online, you will grow that hotel and get the returns you ultimately expected. The key is to have plenty of room for this potential challenge. We call it margin for error.

We purchased an apartment complex at the height of the market in 2007. It struggled for two years. Many tenants were problematic, late payers who trashed the place. Of course, the good tenants became uncomfortable with their neighbors and started leaving the building. Wouldn't you? We had no choice but to address the issue, so over two years, we evicted the problem tenants, renovated those units, and allowed only quality tenants to move in. The building increased cash flow for the next eight years, and we sold it for a substantial gain. The investors did well despite the initial setback.

Good partners work the situation and exercise the control

available to them in order to get the property or project to perform.

A deal may look great on paper, but then you get in and things can change. When the market imploded in 2007, I owned twenty single-family homes that dropped in value by 70 percent seemingly overnight. I couldn't sell them for what I paid for them ten years earlier, but they were all rented out. More people were turning to renting, and so my rental rates increased. What did I care? On paper, I had lost money, but my cash flow still existed. Over time, debt continued to decrease as property values rebounded.

In fact, I took it a step further. I looked around the neighborhoods and bought eight more homes in the area. If I could pick up homes for 30 percent of true value and lease them out, why wouldn't I? I sold my rental homes in early 2017, once fully recovered. I had a solid gain. I hate selling things, and the buyers of these homes will do very well if they operate them correctly. But TIME IS PRECIOUS, and sometimes trading up to larger, easier-to-manage assets can save that precious time.

There are opportunities to make money in either a buyer's or seller's market. You may have temporary setbacks along the way, but both markets can and will change. You just need to be patient and nonreactive.

RESERVES ARE KEY

Cash reserves, or the ability to get cash, are crucial for when opportunities arise. Not many people own all their real estate free and clear. That's not logical. You want to borrow from the bank at around 60 to 70 percent loan to value, depending on the deal. That number is pretty conservative, but the fact is you're going to be better off.

In Michigan, when the market was terrible, vacant buildings sat everywhere. You could buy an office building for cheap, but it was equally important to have the ability to fix up a unit.

Let's say there's a 20,000-square-foot office building for sale, and it's currently vacant. A potential tenant comes along and is willing to pay $12 a square foot to rent the building, plus the tenant will pay all the expenses of the building such as taxes, insurance, utilities, etc. This would provide an annual cash flow of $240,000. You agree to this, but the tenant says they need the inside built out a specific way in order to run their business. You take the architecture plans to a contractor, get a quote, and find out the cost is $300,000. If you don't have the reserves to make these improvements, that potential tenant very well might go elsewhere. Whereas if you have cash on hand, you can fund the build-out and get your property generating very solid cash flow. And you just made that building worth more than $2.4 million!

Is that a revolutionary concept for you? You need cash reserves for opportunities that come along in the markets, and you need cash on hand for temporary setbacks or problems. All of a sudden, a boiler blows or a roof leaks. You need substantial reserves. Again, what's the downside? Having cash on hand means you're not making bad investment choices or jumping into every deal that comes along. NOTE: Make sure whatever deal you are considering has factored in appropriate reserves. You don't have to remember all of this right now. We will provide a list of questions to consider at the end.

A (NOT AMAZON) PRIME EXAMPLE

Borders is a great example of why real estate investment works over putting your money into stocks. The company was launched in Ann Arbor, Michigan—my hometown—by the Borders family. Wonderful people.

Now, if you're old enough to remember, there used to be bookstores everywhere. Unfortunately, they didn't carry all book titles because there wasn't enough space on the shelves. You'd have to go to ten different bookstores, or call around on your rotary phone, to find the book you wanted.

The way I remember it is that Borders came along and revolutionized the space with a warehousing and point-of-sale system that allowed them to offer a larger inventory of books in the same square footage. Instead of keeping a dozen of the same book in stock, they would keep only one or two and replace it as soon as the book sold, bringing in books from a much cheaper warehouse located on the outskirts of town.

This technology gave Borders an advantage over mom-and-pop stores, eventually putting them out of business. Unfortunately, technology changed again. I know you're shocked, right? Online shopping allowed customers to purchase books from an even larger inventory, and often at a discount. The e-reader also provided consumers the ability to purchase a book and immediately read it on their Kindle or iPhone or other device.

I remember standing in a Borders browsing books and then using my phone to instantly buy and download the book. Business over.

Had you invested in Borders stock from the beginning, you would have been rich at one point, and now you'd be broke. Like I said, ALL COMPANIES GO OUT OF BUSINESS EVENTUALLY. The company owed nothing to their investors and didn't have to pay them back. However, had you invested in the buildings Borders occupied, you'd be fine. Borders lasted long enough and paid enough rent, so the buildings they occupied, most very well located, would have been free of any debt by the time Borders eventually closed. The corporate headquarters in downtown Ann Arbor is still around. New tenants pay the owner of the building a handsome amount of rent, even more than when Borders was there. All of the store locations are currently rented and making money.

Here's the lesson: businesses come and go, but real estate remains. If you're the landlord, you keep getting a rent check as long as you have a tenant. No matter what happens, you still own the property. That's why the term is landLORD.

THE ADVANTAGE OF ILLIQUIDITY

I've mentioned repeatedly that there is minimal risk in investing in real estate when done properly, BUT there is one thing you need to be aware of: illiquidity. What does that mean? Let's take a look.

Real estate is not always easy to get out of, especially when the market turns. You may have to accept a lower rate of return for a period of time, and it may be a longer period of time than you were hoping for. You can't snap your fingers and sell a property, which is very different than the immediacy of selling stocks. Stocks are liquid— you can sell them whenever you want. When Volkswagen released news that they had faked their emissions reports, the stock plummeted. People panicked and sold, but if you were a SMART investor, you bought on that bad news, or you stayed put.

That's where the major advantage of real estate investment illiquidity lies. YES, I said the **ADVANTAGE OF ILLIQUIDITY** (that is, the advantage of not being able to sell). This scares a lot of people. If you have a stock and it's not doing well, you can sell whenever you want. Many people do not invest in deals with us because they don't want their money tied up for three, five, or even ten years. It's not even the time that scares them so much as the fact that they can't just snap their fingers and sell their investment if they get worried.

The problem with a liquid investment is that you're more prone to act on emotion. If you get scared or panicked, the urge to just sell and back out is strong even though your best bet is usually to sit on the investment and be patient—especially in real estate investments. No matter what, the level of returns will improve if the property is properly managed, well-located, and purchased correctly—meaning below market value AND below replacement costs.

In 2008, when the market crashed, I could have panicked and sold all of the homes I owned. It's what most people did with the stock market, but I didn't have the option with the properties I owned. I had loans against the houses, so not only would I have lost money in the sales, but there was also a significant chance I would have had to write a check to the bank to pay off the balance because I owed more on them than they were actually worth in that terrible market.

Plus, I had renters, income, and a balance sheet. The bank didn't care what the values of the homes were and I had no other options, so I held on to the properties. Human nature is to sell when things drop. You want to get out of something if the going gets rough...but that causes further panic. Most people do the opposite of what they should, which is to buy when they should sell, and sell when they should buy.

The illiquidity of real estate takes those concerns out of your hands. You have to buy it and hold it, or you have to build it and sell it. If there is bad news, you hang on to the properties. You almost can't get out, and there's no point in doing so. You remain logical because it doesn't make sense to sell homes when you're not going to make a profit. Why would you do that, especially if you're making monthly income in keeping the property? Your capital may evaporate on paper temporarily, but it will come back if you're smart about how you do things—it is cyclical.

In the height of the economic downturn and corresponding widespread panic, I realized I needed to be buying, so I did. You would have been buying as well, IF you were connected to and working with a solid real estate investment partner. Let's talk about how to find someone like that.

Chapter Two

Finding the Right Partner

As a deal sponsor, I spend about two hours every single day talking with current or potential investors—who mostly find us through direct referral or maybe off a podcast or by searching the internet. We have grown almost exclusively by direct referral, so if you didn't know one of my immediate friends or family members, you wouldn't have been able to find us. I CAN'T do what I do without investment dollars, so it's part of my job to go out and look for that money. Having said that, most deal sponsors will not reach out to you. It's impossible because if they reach out to you, you will think it's a scam. Unless you personally know someone great who does this for a living, you are going to have to look around. You have to seek them out.

WHY IS IT *MY (YOUR)* OBLIGATION TO FIND A PARTNER?

Finding the right partner is critical to successfully investing in real estate. Like I've said multiple times (and I'll keep repeating it): *the deal's sponsor is far more important than the deal itself.* So many unforeseen challenges can pop up in any deal. You want someone on your side who understands the challenges you'll face and can predict them before they happen.

The thing is, only a small percentage of deal sponsors have the ability and track record that you'll want and need in a partner. Of those who do, most of them will not seek you out. Why? Because the good ones won't need to. They are too busy looking for deals for their current investors and don't need to search out new ones. The ones who find you are probably not the ones you want to invest with. They tend to approach investors in a "sales-y" way because they don't know what they're doing, which can—and SHOULD—be a big turnoff for an investor like you.

For us, most of our investors come through direct referrals from our existing investors. I (it was just me in the beginning) started with just seven investors a LONG time ago. They were friends, family, and people who already knew me. From there, we (it's a team effort now) have organically grown to hundreds of investors because word of mouth spread that we know what we are doing, and we are constantly putting out the message to pass our name along to anyone they know who might be interested. We ask for referrals. When we do have shares available, they usually get filled by our current list or direct referral. It's highly unlikely that we would ever reach out to you because we simply don't have the time or the need to. Plus, how would we find you? All we can do is respond when you reach out to us.

That's why you have to go LOOK for them. Keep reading; it's easier than you think to find them. Maybe they handed you this book?

BEING ACCREDITED

In order to invest with a real estate investment partner and participate in the private placement deals that are the focus of this book (more on this soon), you need to be an accredited investor. Sorry, but that's the way it works. We'll discuss this all in greater detail in Chapter Six, but for now let's take a brief look at what it means to be accredited.

The SEC defines an accredited investor as someone who has an annual income of at least $200,000 ($300,000 if you file jointly with a spouse) and has been making that amount of money for at least the last three years, OR someone who has a net worth of at least $1 million—excluding the equity in their primary residence.

The irony here is that these numbers for income and/or net worth have not been changed in decades. If you don't meet these criteria, keep reading anyway. Or find someone who does meet the criteria and see if they will give you $10 for this book.

MONEY TALKS

Let me share a little secret with you: every single person out there who makes a living creating and running deals, whether it's a developer or a sponsor, needs capital. The small exception are the families who have huge real estate portfolios and don't want or need investors. They aren't reading this book. You are, and deal sponsors need you for capital.

Let's say there's a big developer in your area and you see a sign on their property that says the project is being developed by ABC Company. You might assume the company is self-funded, but if you like the location and the construction, and you think there's money to be made, you should call and ask if they're taking on any new investors. Nine times out of ten, those developers will absolutely take on new investors because they always need capital.

We have nine active projects at the moment that I'm writing this, and we need about $50 million in capital in order to fund them all. I don't have $50 million rattling around in my checking account. Despite my lack of capital, I'm still not going to go out and call people I don't know and ask them to invest with us without a referral from someone. I've never done that in my life. The only time I might call someone is if I already know them and I have a particular deal with a few shares still available. I recently said to one of my investors, "I have an extra three shares on this deal. Do you want one?" He said he'd take them all. Boom—I don't have to call anyone else. The fact is I don't have time to. When I call someone, I'm not doing it to prospect: I spend those two hours on the phone every day calling people who have already invested with me or have been referred to me as a potential investor. If they're not interested, I ask them if they know someone who is. Like everyone else, I need investors.

PROSPECTING FOR MORE THAN JUST GOLD

So, if they're not going to come looking for you, how do you find them?

The answer is prospecting, which is the most important life skill you can cultivate. Prospecting is the process of taking consistent action toward meeting and connecting with people in order to achieve a set goal or fulfill a desire.

Actively focusing on what I want and then allocating a little time each day to finding it, through actively prospecting, has given me everything I've ever asked or looked for. I want for nothing because I went out and found it. Learn more about prospecting; it's PURE GOLD. I learned the skill from Mike Ferry, who coaches real estate agents, but it applies to anything and everything. Go to www.Mike-Ferry.com, get his scripts, and then change the words to whatever you want. Attend an event; it's great for one's mindset. So is Tony Robbins, seriously.

You can get anything you want in life—literally anything—through prospecting. You can get tickets to events, high-quality romantic partners, and even great friends.

And deal sponsors. You need financial opportunities in order to live free from any financial constraints.

PICK UP THE PHONE

Prospecting requires picking up the phone (or starting a face-to-face conversation) and talking to people. Pick up the phone or open up your email, and say or write, "I'm an accredited investor looking for real estate deals. Do you happen to know anyone who puts deals together?" If you contacted ten people in this manner, you'd likely find a deal to get in on. Or, more likely, about twenty deals.

So, who to ask?

Talk to friends and colleagues about any successful real estate investing they've done and with whom. If you're a member of a country club, for example, there are likely at least a few other members who have invested in a real estate deal. You might even find your sponsor through a real estate agent you know. In our Ann Arbor market, a lot of realtors know us because we're a great resource for them when their clients want to get into real estate investing.

Most everyone uses the doctor. I can tell you from experience that doctors are huge real estate investors—we have at least seventy doctors invested in our various funds. Next time you're in a doctor's office, say, "Hey, doc, I know this is off topic—and I really appreciate you taking a look at my (blank)—but I was just curious: have you ever invested in any real estate deals or know anybody who puts them together? I'm interested in getting started, but I don't know of any good sponsors." Notice the differentiation there: make it clear that you're not looking for good *deals* necessarily, you're looking for good *people*.

Professional organizations, large and small, are also a good place for prospecting and referrals. I do a ton of stuff, like coaching my kid's flag football team and baseball team as well as taking karate with my daughter. I meet people there, and I can ask them anything I want to. It leads to all sorts of opportunities.

TAKE A DRIVE

Another form of prospecting is simply driving around and checking out new construction. Let's say you see a condominium being built that you'd like to invest in. Call the developer and say, "Hey, I like your project in Ann Arbor. I'm not interested in buying one of the condos, but I'm really interested in knowing if you accept investors into your projects in general."

That's all you have to ask. Hopefully, they're not idiots and they'll be happy to get you on their list, send you their deals, or even ask you to come in for a meeting. They'll ask questions, of course, like "What kind of capital are you looking to invest? Are you looking for cash flow? Are you looking for long-term appreciation?" As we know, questions are a good thing.

KEEP YOUR EYES AND EARS OPEN

Be open and aware. You may find the right sponsor from a podcast you listen to, or a book they wrote, or at a speaking engagement. Pick up the phone and call them.

HELPING PEOPLE HELPS YOU

This is one of my favorite referral stories. I met a guy named Bill (fake name, real story), and he was in debt up to his eyeballs. His company, ACME Electric (not his actual business name, real story), wasn't making any money, and somehow he got my name and he called me for advice. I helped Bill create a business plan and provided him with a few scripts to use with customers and prospects.

Two years later he called me to invest some money in one of our deals. I thought he might have ten grand saved up for a deal, maybe a little more. I said, "How much do you want to place?"

He said, "My accountant told me I really need to take $500,000 out of the business and put it somewhere."

"$500,000?!" I said. "Last time I saw you, your gross sales were $2 million a *year*. You were nearly dead on the vine."

"Oh, no," he said. "We did $20 million last year."

That deal led to several referrals, and now members of Bill's family also invest with me. Bill flies all over the country talking to people about me because I helped him. That, in turn, continues to lead to more calls from new potential investors because of his word of mouth. To be clear, I didn't really do that much; he did the work and made his business what it is today. But I did what I could at the time, and he's smart—really smart. He knows it's easier to make money with our deals than to go out and buy his own buildings.

HOW *NOT* TO FIND THE RIGHT PARTNER

You can find deals elsewhere, but nothing beats direct referrals. In some cases, finding deals elsewhere can in fact be a bad thing.

On the internet, for example, you can find information on deals. In my experience, though, most new investors wouldn't know the difference between a good deal and a bad deal just by reading a private placement memorandum. They're long, dense packets of legal information. For someone like me, who has reviewed hundreds of these deals, they seem simple. The way to use the internet correctly, in this context, would be as a tool to contact knowledgeable people.

Like the internet, local real estate organizations would seem like a good place to turn, but they're often just promotional ventures. What I mean by that is yes, you might be able to contact a local real estate agent who helps people with income properties. That agent might help you find a property to buy as a real estate investment, but they're mostly motivated by the commission. Once you buy it, they'll be gone. Use them as a recommendation for a deal sponsor instead.

There are other groups on LinkedIn and Facebook, such as the Accredited Investor Association of America. These might seem like good alternatives, but they're all trying to get something from you, which isn't necessarily a bad thing, but you need to understand people's financial motivations. I don't deny that if you invest in my deals, it's good for me because it allows me to make a living. But with me, that's fully disclosed right up front—nothing's hidden. You know what you're getting out of it, and you know what I'm getting out of it. That's the way I think it should be. Just know that not everybody will operate with full disclosure.

TRANSPARENCY

Speaking of disclosure, if you find a potential deal sponsor (or anybody in investing) who's not willing to be 100 percent transparent with you, then you've found someone you'd be better off not dealing with. Sponsors may not be fully transparent online, but when you interview them and ask questions, they need to answer with full disclosure.

Think about it like going to the doctor. You say, "Hey, doc, it's great that you want to rip my tonsils out and all, but I'm twenty-two years old, and this is the first issue I've ever had with them. What makes you think I really need to have this surgery?" When the doctor insists on surgery because he makes more money on it than a round of antibiotics that will likely clear up an infection, you would probably consider getting a second opinion.

It's the same with investing. If a potential investor came to me and said, "How do you guys get paid on the deal?" I'd have an answer. The question is familiar, and the answer is that there are several different ways (sometimes we get a developer fee or a management fee along the way, but most of our compensation is through equity written into the deals). I always explain this to our investors, and it is fully disclosed.

Don't get caught up on how much your sponsor is making—that's not the point. The point is, does the value they create justify giving them that cut? And in what order does the money come out of the deal?

BEWARE INDUSTRY WEB PORTALS

Another place to find deals is through industry web portals, but beware. The real estate investing industry has yet to produce a good crowdfunding model. There are portals such as RealtyShares and RealtyMogul, but the problem with them is that they don't actually connect the investor to the deal sponsor. They act as middlemen, putting a sponsor's deal on their website and attempting to raise money from investors. Those investors, however, will never have an opportunity to speak directly to someone like me, the sponsor. I wouldn't participate in a deal like that if I were an investor because you have no way of calling and talking to the deal sponsor to get a feel for who they are. You can't ask all those important questions.

Web portals are more like a broker connection. The sites tout high-return deals, so an investor often takes a shotgun approach: investing $10,000 each into ten different deals. As the sponsor, though, I don't know my investors. That's bad. There's something that clicks in people's heads when the other side of a deal is blind to them. Like when you rent a car, it's more likely you treat it like crap than if you borrowed a car from a friend. Why? Because the rental car company is just some big corporation. Once you put a curtain up between sponsors and investors, the sponsors are more inclined to run around putting deals together just to make their fees. This happens because they're not making connections with people. When was the last time you took your rental car through a car wash?

PROSPECT EVEN IF YOU'RE NOT READY

Let's say you're not accredited. It doesn't mean you can't seek out deal sponsors and learn about potential investments. Don't be proud of your ignorance. Try things out and learn about them. I always tell people, "Don't say 'I can't afford it.' If it's something you really want in life, don't tell yourself you can't have it." The same thing is true of real estate investing. Even if you can't afford to get into a deal right now, it's still good to learn about the process and test-drive it, so to speak. The connections you make now will pay off later when you are accredited, literally.

In fact, this is normal. We have about 1,000 people on our potential investor list who don't meet the investor criteria. Fine—we don't care. They can still see every deal we send out, and they can call us and ask questions. I'll spend time with these people because they're learning and gaining knowledge. Someday, when they do have the capital, they'll have the experience and knowledge to get in on a deal. You never know when life will bring you some money—a lot sooner if you are actively looking for it.

I have investors who were dead broke but stayed on our list for years. One man, a lawyer, lost a lot of money in the real estate downturn (not on my deals, for the record). Although he wasn't accredited, he continued to review PPM deals. Eventually, he got a substantial payout in a class action lawsuit, and immediately he was an accredited investor. If he hadn't stayed on our list and continued to pay attention, he wouldn't have been prepared when that money came his way.

What I'm saying is even if you're not accredited yet, get on investor lists and give it a test drive to see if you're really interested in this process. Worst-case scenario? You learn more and you're prepared for when money does come your way.

Accredited or not accredited, the point here is that deal sponsors will not seek you out—you have to find them. People need capital, and if you can provide it, that's a valuable asset.

REMEMBER: IT'S ABOUT THE PEOPLE

You have to prospect for good *people* as opposed to only good *deals*. Finding a great deal sponsor might seem easy at first. Make sure you are:

1. Taking the initiative to find a great real estate sponsor.
2. Keeping your eyes open to what's going on in your market and in the cities that you visit—ideally NOT resort or seasonal locations but real working cities with cranes in the air.
3. Helping others and then NOT being afraid to ask them to help you—remember this? "Hey, Bill (or whoever), who do you know that creates solid investment opportunities?"
4. Working with someone who operates with transparency.
5. STAYING AWAY from ANYTHING you are not 100 percent comfortable with.

Chapter Three

Starting Out and Moving Forward

If you've found a deal sponsor you want to partner with, start *slowly* with them—don't invest a huge percentage of your capital on any one deal, especially your first one. Allocate 5, maybe 10 percent of your invested capital on one deal. The absolute maximum would be 20 percent. You just don't want that money locked up until you know a few very important things. Test it out and see how things go with this particular sponsor. It's possible that it could be a great deal and that you've found a fantastic person to invest with. If not, you will want to have some staying power. Remember, if a deal is solid, the only problems you run into are temporary setbacks that can be bridged if you have the cash available to back them up. You can never have enough money in the best deals, and you always have too much in the bad ones.

WHAT SHOULD I LOOK FOR OVER TIME?

Check your comfort level with your new deal sponsor. How they communicate with you and how often is very important. Whether it's monthly, quarterly, or semiannually, by email, snail mail, or conference calls, ask yourself if they're sticking to their communication plan. You certainly don't want to hear from them daily, because that's just not how real estate evolves. In my experience, daily reports are prone to causing overreaction, and reporting takes time. What are they doing if they are talking to you all the time?

Most of the time, what we hear from our investors is crickets—that is, nothing. And that's a good thing because it means we're reporting the right amount of information to them and they're happy with the news they're hearing. As an investor, if you're not happy with the way your sponsor is reporting to you, you should mention it. As of the writing of this book, I'd expect to hear from a sponsor by email. The phone is almost obsolete unless they notice that emails are going unopened, in which case they may call to make sure they aren't going into a spam folder.

How and what they communicate will tell you if they're

truthful and how they approach problems. Before you invest, ask for examples of past communications with investors, and make sure you're comfortable with them. Did they give conservative estimates? You can look back and see if they originally projected a 20 percent return and then see what the actual results were. Was the sponsor transparent with their updates, and did they address challenges that a particular deal faced? When the deal comes to fruition, the ultimate test is to see whether you want to invest with someone again. There are lots of things to consider, as I'll talk about in a minute, but for now, the most important question to ask yourself is this: did this deal meet the projections?

If the answer is yes, then you ask if your new partner reported to you well. Did the sponsor make a consistent effort throughout the project to manage it the right way and handle all the details and unexpected situations? Because in any market, even with something as stable as real estate, there are elements beyond anyone's control. Even the most experienced sponsors can put together a deal that doesn't work out.

You also have to look at the trends surrounding the deals. If you happened to get into an investment in 2006, it wouldn't matter how good the deal and the sponsor were because the whole world imploded in 2007. You might've said that you only broke even when the deal was supposed to return 15 percent, but during that time, what was the stock market doing? It was dropping significantly. Performance is relative. A great sponsor won't make deals during those times because it would be like trying to find a needle in a haystack. Partner with someone who keeps it simple. If you're a novice investor, a good sponsor should be able to explain their deal in a way you understand. And once you find a deal sponsor who consistently under-promises and over-delivers, then you can think about investing a larger percentage of your capital with them.

START SMART

You need to ask yourself the earlier questions about meeting projections and your relationship with your sponsor, but you also want to go into a deal confident that you'll like the answers. So always start by looking for the safe deals. Always start with, "What is the downside?" Of course, you can lose all your money in the deal, but what's the likelihood of that happening? What are you relying on? If the deal is building condominiums at a certain price and selling them for a profit, then find out how that's quantified. Does the information provided to you include a copy of the GMP (gross maximum price) contract with the builder (aka general contractor)? Is there a contingency fee in the number for overages? On the flip side, who else is selling completed condominiums in that market, and what are they getting price-wise? The smartest investors I've ever seen are interested in PRESERVATION OF CAPITAL. Yes, they want a return, but they are more interested in the return of their capital than in a super high yield. The reason for this is simple. If you put $100,000 in five different deals ($500,000 total) and you hit 20 percent return on four of them and lose your money on one of them, you still have $500,000. I'd rather make a solid 10 percent on all of them and end up with $550,000.

There are an endless number of deals out there—a good sponsor will keep finding them for a long time. Work once to find that great partner, and get paid forever. You don't have to put all your eggs into one deal. There will always be more deals.

PATIENCE IS A (MONEYMAKING) VIRTUE

Your next step after you've put money into a deal? Be patient. Ask questions (if you have any) and watch what happens. You don't have to be uber aggressive. Just sit back and watch. The smartest investors I've met are the most patient. This is where the advantage of illiquidity comes into play. They see the world as their laboratory. They watch how other people work as well as analyze how they conduct themselves. Over time, patient investors will decide to commit more money in areas that make sense and move it away from ventures that aren't working. They focus on avoiding losing at all costs instead of chasing high returns on some home run deal. They're not interested in that. Smart investors are interested in the safe, predictable deal that gives them a fair return.

FIND THE RIGHT HORSE, AND KEEP BETTING ON IT

Developers from all over the country are constantly bringing us projects that they need capital for. When we find a potentially good developer, we typically start small with them to separate the wheat from the chaff. If that small initial deal goes well, we'll greenlight the next project with them and do more. It's the same way I suggest you vet for good deal sponsors.

I have one broker in Michigan who brought me a deal back in '09. Since then, we've made at least twenty acquisitions through him, adding up to about $150 million in real estate deals alone—all through one broker. With a 2 to 3 percent commission, he's earned some nice money on those deals. Every single one of those deals has worked out. He represents things fairly, openly, and honestly, which is especially hard to find in a real estate broker. We don't try to chisel at his commission; we see the value in the deals he brings us and we pay him for it.

That's the same way you should look at the process of finding a deal sponsor. Someone who's protecting your net worth above and beyond what's in it for them is very valuable to you. Once you find the right horse, you keep betting on it—there's no reason not to. It's why we keep working with that same broker and the same developers, and it's why you should find a good sponsor and keep working with them.

In addition to brokers coming to us with investment ideas, we also know non-brokers who know how to go out and find deals. We put up the money, and they handle the lease or renovation or whatever it may take to reposition the property. We have one guy who we've completed two deals with so far, and we're looking at three more. He's a street fighter. He knows how to go out, find deals, and get them under contract at the right price. We handle the money and the accounting; he handles what needs to be done to the property. When we sell it, he gets a huge piece of that pie and makes a ton of money. On one deal alone, his side of the deal made $3.4 million upon the sale of the asset, which was two years after we bought it. He didn't put in a penny of his own money. He also made management, leasing, and construction management fees along the way, which works out to another couple hundred grand per year. What I'm trying to say is that I don't begrudge anyone making money while they're in the process of making me money. And you shouldn't either.

Part of the idea of doing the work once and getting paid forever is finding a collection of people to surround yourself with who you can mutually support. This applies to far more than just real estate deals. If you find a great doctor, you cherish that relationship and you might send him more business from friends and family. If you find a great assistant, you create a mutual loyalty. You keep going back to these people. People do business with people they like. In Ann Arbor, I know about five different restaurant owners personally, and I frequent their restaurants. The service is great, I like them, and it's way better than eating at a chain restaurant. Is that worth paying a little extra? Absolutely. If you enjoy the benefits, it shouldn't matter if the person providing value is making a little money along the way, as long as the value is there for you too.

THE 20 PERCENT RULE

I try to limit my investors to having 20 percent or less of their total capital invested with me, but I know many of them have much more than 20 percent invested. Personally, I keep about 80 percent of my capital in my own deals. I don't invest in the stock market much. I think my choice to keep that much money in our deals is a vote of confidence in our investments. It says that I won't do deals just to do them—I believe in them.

Generally speaking, I'd say you should put no more than

20 percent of your total capital in any type of asset. If I have someone tell me they have all of their retirement money in the stock market, I tell them to find someone who understands real estate investing and give them some of your capital. If you have $2 million in retirement funds, you should work your way up to having $400,000 in real estate investments with a sponsor you trust and break that up into four or five different deals.

Most people who put a huge chunk of their capital into real estate deals either owned a rental property themselves or had a family member who owned them. Either way, it's often the case that they have some experience, whether firsthand or secondhand, and understand that process more than a purely passive investor. These people who heavily invest in real estate have confidence with it. I compare it to having a mortgage on a house. Some people have a million-dollar house with a $400,000 mortgage on it, and they're comfortable with that. Other people would be comfortable with a $900,000 mortgage on that same home. For me, I don't want a mortgage or any debt of any kind on assets that I own personally. Similarly, in real estate investment you have to pick the comfort level you have in order to decide what percentage to invest. When you're in that comfort zone, it means you won't panic, and that's good, because panic leads to bad decisions.

When it comes to asset allocation, I'm more interested

in percentage of net worth rather than dollar amounts. If you're just starting out, my advice to you is to get a cash reserve before anything else, especially if you don't have any savings already. That will be your rainy day fund. Then, start consistently allocating some of it to different asset classes. A good formula would be 25 percent to real estate deals, 25 percent toward an index fund, 25 percent in cash, and 25 percent in personal debt reduction. Once all personal debt is gone, increase the other three categories.

THE VALUE OF RELATIONSHIPS

I'm not a financial advisor, but my longest-term investor is my dad. He's been investing with me for about twenty years. He didn't put money in my first deal back in 1998—he just cosigned on the loan—but I still gave him 50 percent of the returns and he made a lot of money on it. However, I don't normally recommend investing with your kids—I've seen it go wrong too many times. My dad is happy: he's retired, and he doesn't have to worry about money anymore. But it doesn't always work that way. I've seen other fathers invest in their kids' ventures and have to bail them out. It can totally ruin the kid's self-esteem. I'm adamant that I don't bail out my children. They will fall and hurt themselves and have to experience failure and setbacks. They know I love them, and I want them to feel safe, but they also need to stand on their own two feet. Full disclosure: my kids are ages six to twelve right now, so there's a solid chance that I might cave on this philosophy someday.

I encourage others to take that same attitude when it comes to investing. If you want to help a family member with a venture, I say don't help with money—help them learn how to invest the right way. Over the years I've gotten calls from people who say their son or daughter is opening a restaurant or other business venture, and they ask me what I think of them putting a few hundred grand in the deal. No, no, no. I'll tell them to have their kid come meet with me and I'll teach them how to put a business prospectus together. Going through the exercise of creating the kind of deal I'm teaching and advocating for in this book, and trying to raise the money in smaller chunks, will teach them a valuable skill. Maybe the parent puts in $25 or $50 thousand to get them going, but no more than 10 to 20 percent of what's needed for the venture. Make them work for it. **No one has ever learned more from being given something than they would have learned by doing it on their own.**

A good relationship is one you don't take advantage of. I have mentors and high net worth investors that I could call up and get $5 million from in twenty-five minutes, if I needed it. However, I would never take advantage of those relationships. The reason I have the ability to call in those favors is because I've never taken advantage of my relationships with people. The reason my dad continues to invest with me is because I've provided him with value over the last twenty years. I've never taken advantage of the same generosity in him that led him to cosign on my first loan. He's not just money to me, and you shouldn't just be money to a sponsor. When selecting a deal sponsor, make sure it's someone who sees you as a valuable person, not just money.

Chapter Four

The Right Deal and
Deal Philosophy

Real estate is not an industry with dramatic new insights, and it doesn't reward showmanship. If a deal sounds too complicated, then it probably is, and therefore it is just flat out not worth investing in, for a myriad of reasons. You don't need to get lost in tax law, depreciation, or the specific deal structure—remember, that's why you spent all that time finding the right sponsor.

PERSONAL VS. PUBLIC VS. PRIVATE INVESTING

Before we move forward, it's time to get a bit technical. We're going to visit all this in more detail in Chapter Seven, but for now it's important to have a basic understanding of the kinds of real estate investing out there so that you know you're making the smart choice.

Those looking to invest in real estate have three different options: personal, public, and private investing. I'll walk you through each briefly so you can see why private deals, the PPMs that are the focus of this book, are the way to go. And it's important to know why some of the other options, even if they seem attractive, might not be a good fit for you.

DIRECT INVESTING

Many people choose to invest directly into real estate on their own, buying property themselves as an investment other than their primary residence. A lot of people do this and do much of the work on their own. It can be done. You can buy a single property as an investment, rent it out, and manage everything on your own. You can purchase a piece of land you think will increase in value. You can even buy a vacation property—which, for the record, is usually a HORRIBLE idea. They're not typically a moneymaker—they're usually more of an investment in your ego than anything else.

With direct investing, you can't typically do as well as you can with a deal sponsor because it can take years and years to build the experience needed for success. And even then, most people don't factor in time (our most precious asset) and what they could be spending that time on if they weren't dealing with the massive amount of details involved with real estate. It's a second job. You're not doing the work once and getting paid forever; you're doing the work forever.

PUBLIC REITS

Another way individuals invest in real estate is through a public REIT, or real estate investment trust. Traded on Wall Street, REITs are usually asset-specific, meaning they focus on one asset class like apartment buildings or industrial buildings, but there are also diversified REITs that contain multiple types of assets. For example, Apple (not the Apple that makes your phone or computer) is a REIT that purchases, owns, and operates hotels. If the economy is doing great and more people are traveling (thus staying in hotels), you might want to invest in the hospitality sector and a company like Apple. There are even REITs for manufactured home communities (also known as trailer parks), meaning there are big publicly traded companies that own gobs and gobs of manufactured home communities. (A man by the name of Sam Zell, a billionaire real estate professional, created REITs for a living. He has an excellent book called *Am I Being Too Subtle? Straight Talk from a Business Rebel*, which I encourage you to read if you want to know more about REITs.)

PRIVATE PLACEMENT MEMORANDUMS

Another way to invest is through private placement memorandums, and these are the focus of this book. A private placement memorandum, or PPM, is a legal document provided to prospective investors when selling shares of a real estate deal. A PPM is used in "private" transactions as opposed to public transactions, which are heavily monitored by the SEC. The PPM describes the deal sponsor, the terms of the offering, and the risks of the investment, among other things.

PPMs can be used to raise money for a single property deal, like an apartment complex, or PPMs can have a fund structure where money is raised for a portfolio of properties. Companies that follow a fund structure may own dozens of buildings or have a portfolio of development deals within a fund. The PPM is supposed to disclose ALL THE KNOWN RISKS of the deal and spell out how everyone gets paid. READ IT! If it smells fishy or isn't clear, then ask questions or AVOID the deal.

WHAT SHOULD I LOOK FOR IN A PPM REAL ESTATE DEAL?

When you get into a deal, focus on the fundamentals. You want to understand the basics of a deal, but it's easy to be paralyzed by analysis. Don't focus on nickels and dimes. Focus on whether or not this is a good project in a good location. Focus on how money flows in and out of the deal. And if you've found the right sponsor, the smaller details shouldn't be an issue.

The PPM should say exactly what has been represented to you. While the PPM will have a tremendous amount of scary legal disclosures, if you focus on the money water-fall, how people get paid, and other deal fundamentals (more on this in a moment), you will confirm that you've found the right deal sponsor—or not.

And remember, if you have questions about any of it, you shouldn't be afraid to ask. It's okay to get scared off a few times. You will eventually get used to reading PPMs and gain a comfort level with them.

WHAT ARE DEAL FUNDAMENTALS?

So what are these deal fundamentals? They're the basic steps and concepts of how a deal is put together. It's the big picture. As an investor, what you *don't* need to get caught up in is the nitty-gritty details of things like tax law, depreciation, and the finer analysis of a deal's structure—unless you have that kind of time and it's how you want to spend it. So, let's take a look at some of these basics.

SPONSOR FEE FOR OVERHEAD

Typically, a deal sponsor will get reasonable developer fees along the way in order to cover their time and overhead. What qualifies as reasonable? It depends on the size of the deal and how much time and energy it will require on the part of the sponsor.

I tend to think about it like this: by the time the PPM comes out to investors, the sponsor has probably spent six months to a year getting it to the point that it's ready to go. That's a lot of pro bono work. The most important thing here is that everything is transparent and there are no hidden fees. Don't be afraid to ask, "What's this fee? Who's it going to? And why?"

THE BANK GETS PAID FIRST

The bank should be the first entity to get paid back when a deal liquidates. On a construction loan, the bank will be paid 100 percent of the proceeds from the sale of all the units until they've been paid back. That's just how it works.

WHEN AND HOW YOU (SHOULD) GET PAID

Then it's your turn: the equity investors should be paid back next. The real cash (aka the investors' money) should always get preferential treatment, meaning they get paid back before the deal sponsor shares in any additional profits. There are a lot of different ways of splitting the profits at the end of a deal. Sometimes you'll see investors who get 6 to 8 percent "preferred return" per annum on their money—I've even seen it as high as 18 percent.

Here's how it should work. Let's say, for example, that I need $4 million from investors and $6 million from the bank. Upon liquidating the deal (i.e., selling the property), the bank gets their $6 million back first, you get your $4 million back second, then we'll distribute the profits in the form of preferred returns to the investors, which can be very small or very large depending on the deal. Then we split the excess profits (usually 50/50, but this can vary as well).

On deals that have a chance for huge returns, you'll often see a higher *preferred* return to the investor, say 15 percent annually, but the investor will get a smaller amount of the additional profits above and beyond that, say 10 to 15 percent. The reason for structuring a big deal like this is because the sponsor likely thinks this particular deal has a chance of getting a massive return. Therefore, they are willing to completely back-end their portion of the profit and almost guarantee you a solid 15 percent return in exchange for them getting a huge upside at the end of the deal.

That's just one example. Another example, which is more typical, involves a 6 to 8 percent preferred return. This type of deal would usually give the investor a bigger portion of the excess return at the end of the deal—like a 50/50 split. On one hand, the investors are risking hard-earned dollars and should have a chance for the higher returns these types of deals can get you. On the other hand, getting the first 12 to 15 percent out of a deal and a smaller upside piece can be justified as well.

I've seen fair deals on all parts of the spectrum—neither of these examples of deal structures should be red flags for you. The structure is just another piece of information to take into account when you decide whether or not to get into a deal.

GETTING PAID: A QUICK RECAP

So, generally speaking, the waterfall of how the money flows when a deal liquidates looks like this:

1. Bank gets paid back
2. Original investor capital is returned
3. Investor capital receives a preferred return on their investment
4. The remaining profits are split up between the deal sponsor and the investors

BEING SMART

Don't forget the rule of thumb for real estate investing: the sexier the deal, the worse it probably is. There are several important points to keep in mind when considering a deal.

THE BIG GUNS IN TOWN

In the Wild West of real estate investing, everybody wants to be the big gun in town. You want to steer clear of these gunslingers (i.e., chest-pounding, inexperienced, flashy guys who act like they know everything and are typically most concerned with making large sums of money for themselves). These guys may talk a good game and have a sexy-looking investor prospectus, but most of the time, the numbers in their deals will be full of unrealistic projections that will ultimately cause their deals to fail.

You can identify these guys because they will always be selling, selling, selling. They're talking big sums with just as big optimism. They should make you step back and think, "Wait. What's the reality of this deal? Can they boil it down to me in layman's terms?"

The good sponsors will tell you why they like the deal, why they think it will make money, and what's on the potential upside AND downside. Of course, we can't know for sure how an investment will perform, so the good sponsors will use conservative numbers.

Preserving your capital is very important. Chasing high yields (gambling) is not something you want to get into with real estate investing. Remember, if a deal sounds too good to be true, it probably is. PPM deals should be safe, secure, and boring. The big gun guys, on the other hand, will be all flash and no cash. If it were possible to create deals that made ridiculous returns, then they wouldn't need you for more than the first one, right? They'd be able to make so much money that they could just work with the profits from their first deal.

ROSY PROJECTIONS

One thing you want to look at when considering investments is the ratio of cash to debt. For example, a common tactic you'll see is using mezzanine lenders. On a $10 million deal, let's say the sponsor has a $7.5 million loan from the primary lender, then he's got a secondary source (called a mezzanine lender) loaning $1.5 million on the deal. Look out for secondary lenders like this—they're predatory. The sponsor will need only another $1 million in cash, just 10 percent, to complete the deal. They'll tell you that you're going to get twenty times your money because they're over-leveraging with bank debt. I typically recommend sticking with no more than 75 percent total leverage, but less debt is even better. Forty percent equity to 60 percent debt is a pretty conservative ratio.

Over-leveraging can be shaky ground to stand on. There's no reason to do it unless you don't know how to raise money correctly or if you're trying to hit a home run in your first at bat in the major leagues. You don't need home runs in this industry—you need a lot of base hits. Take your singles, take your doubles, and occasionally you'll hit one hard and it'll make it over the wall.

In addition to conservative leverage, you'll also want to make sure there's enough of a cash reserve in the deal to take care of unforeseen expenses. These reserves, or contingencies, will just be cash held in an account for cost overruns, vacancies, capital expenditures, or other expenses associated with owning or developing real estate.

GET THE RIGHT SPONSOR (WITH ENOUGH MONEY)

Have I mentioned yet that finding a good sponsor you can trust is the most important thing? Well, I'll say it again. *You have to find the right sponsor.*

If the sponsor acts as the loan guarantor, the bank will qualify them and get a personal financial statement, tax returns, and just about everything else in the world to verify they have some money to back the deal. That is likely enough in terms of knowing if they have any net worth or cash at risk.

If the debt is non-recourse (more on this in just a moment), then your deal sponsor should have no problem answering the question "What's your net worth?" Not everyone will give you that level of detail on their finances, but they should give you some idea that they have more than two pennies to rub together if they're asking you to put $50,000, or a lot more, in a deal. At the same time, the sponsor has his job because he needs to make money and make a living. You can't expect them to not need your money—if they didn't need it, then you wouldn't have an opportunity to invest anyway.

In the end, you're collecting all of this information on a deal so you can answer the question "Should I invest in this?" If you don't feel like it's 100 percent yes, then it's a no—a philosophy to apply to everything you can in life.

TWO TYPES OF LOANS

There are two types of debt: recourse and non-recourse. I've been talking about this a bit already. As an investor, the reason you want to know whether a deal is recourse or non-recourse is because, first of all, a non-recourse loan means your deal sponsor is *not* on the hook for the loan. Therefore, his commitment to the project might not be quite as strong as on a recourse loan deal, where the sponsor is personally guaranteeing the loan. Let's look at both types in more detail.

RECOURSE

Recourse debt requires someone who the bank deems worthy to personally guarantee the debt. If the bank loans that money against an apartment complex that you're buying, and you run that complex into the ground, the bank uses the personal guarantee as collateral if you don't make enough money to pay the loan back. They chase the guarantor.

Most deals, whether acquisitions or developments, require some level of bank financing. With a $10 million deal, for example, if you're using $3 million in investor cash and you're getting the other $7 million from the bank, the bank will typically want a guarantee on that loan. If the sponsor is the personal guarantor, the bank has the right to pursue that person individually to make up for a shortfall in cash. Also, if the bank takes the property back, liquidates it (because they have the right to do that), and sells it for $5 million, then the personal guarantor owes them $2 million. They have the right to go after your personal assets to make up for that $2 million difference. That's why I say to NEVER invest in a deal where the sponsor asks you, the investor, to be on the loan with them!

NON-RECOURSE

A non-recourse loan means the bank will still take the apartment complex, or non-performing asset, but they have nobody to go after on the loan except for what are called "bad-boy carve-outs," which is another phrase for fraudulent sponsors. The bank won't pursue the sponsor personally for the shortfall between the $7 million borrowed and whatever loss they wound up selling the property for, unless the sponsor committed fraud or did something illegal. With non-recourse loans, all the lender can do is take the property.

With a recourse loan, if the deal sponsor is personally on the hook for the loan and the deal's going bad, that sponsor will dig in and give it everything they have because they may have to come out of pocket with their own money if they don't fix it. Whereas on a non-recourse loan, the sponsor could just wash their hands of it all and give the property back to the bank. In this scenario, the investors lose their money, but the sponsor's not out anything.

There are arguments for, or against, both types of loans. For example, I could say it's better to have a non-recourse loan because if a deal went bad, it gives us more negotiating power with the lender, since they're not likely to just take the property back. Lenders aren't set up to manage real estate assets or development projects, so the last thing they want is for a deal sponsor to default on a non-recourse loan. When this happens, a non-recourse lender is more likely to work with the deal sponsor to try to save the deal (e.g., forgive a portion of the debt, lengthen amortization periods, switch the loan to interest only, etc.) than they are to take the property back. The most important thing to know is which type of deal you're making, because it's another piece of the puzzle that tells you a bit more about the sponsor.

It's unusual for people to lose more money than they invest in a deal, but it does happen, especially to athletes. Somehow, they get convinced to put their name on the personal guarantee for recourse debt. This also seems to happen a lot with restaurants. You don't want to invest a dollar and potentially lose two. You should be able to limit your losses to your invested capital if a deal goes south, then ask yourself what you learned from this and move on to the next opportunity. Last time I'll say it, and I hope you've got this one—as an investor, you should NEVER be a personal guarantor for the debts of the company you are investing in. Make sure your losses are limited to your initial investment. The company may have the right to make a capital call (ask for more money if there's a problem or shortfall), but this shouldn't be mandatory.

MY UNDERLYING PHILOSOPHY

Successful real estate investing begins with a conservative, consistent deal philosophy. Real estate cycles tend to be long-term, generally twenty to thirty years. I'm not a stock guy. I'm not a bond guy. There are guys like Warren Buffett who can buy companies and make money—that's great. For me, I prefer real estate and its long-term cycles. I like taking advantage of its stable and predictable nature, and I try to utilize that in order to generate income or capital growth. I have no interest in anything that feels like gambling. Once an investor has taken the time to talk to me (or my team) and get their questions answered—basically getting them accustomed to everything we do—they know they've found the right person (or not) to invest with. That's what it means to do the work once and get paid forever.

The work is in finding the right people. For you, an investor reading this book, I'll say it again: spend your time and energy learning about a specific deal sponsor. You can trust that they'll tell you the best times to buy and sell. Why? Because they almost always have their own money at stake in these deals. At the very least, the sponsor's financial interests should be aligned with yours. A good partner can help you generate consistent income no matter what phase of the real estate cycle we're in.

THE REAL ESTATE CYCLE

If you don't understand how the real estate cycle works and what stage it's in, then you're not going to be a smart investor. And if your sponsor can't tell you where the cycle is, then it's time to find a new sponsor.

It turns out that when it comes to real estate, history tends to repeat itself. It's not always identical, and there are always hiccups along the way. It's important to know approximately WHERE you are at any given time when it comes to this cycle. A good sponsor may know this, but in many cases they don't. You don't want to be chasing cash flow deals when you are at the peak of the development portion of the cycle, and you don't want to be investing in development deals when the market is about to crash, or even if it's just in the leveling-off period (more on what all that means in a moment). You don't need a crystal ball to understand the cycle, and you don't have to be too precise either. But you do need to be aware.

HOW THE REAL ESTATE CYCLE WORKS

It's very easy to look at history and see cycles in all kinds of things. History repeats itself, as they say, and that is certainly true in real estate.

The real estate cycle varies, but it usually completes itself about every twenty to thirty years. Where to begin? We could begin anywhere—it's a cycle, after all—but let's start our look at the cycle as it's coming out of a downturn.

This is a period of recovery. Prices are rock bottom, and because of that people start buying up assets. The more people buy, the scarcer these assets become. The demand is the same, but the supply is decreasing because nothing new is being constructed, so values (and rents) naturally start to increase. Everything out there—homes, industrial, office space—fills up. (There's a pattern to note here. Usually things begin to be bought or leased in the more affluent communities first, before moving into lower-income and more rural areas.)

Now that everything is full, there's no (or very little) supply. Prices are now high. They're so high, in fact, that it costs just about as much to build as it does to buy something existing. So now developers are building new property. Now we're into the development cycle. It takes a few years for development to really ramp up.

It's important (and interesting) to note how this affects the rest of the economy, and how that in turn affects real estate. All this building creates more jobs than you might think. Suddenly title companies, architects, engineers, and surveyors all need more office space. Window and roof companies are installing more windows and roofs. And therefore wholesalers are selling more windows and shingles. It adds all kinds of new job creation. It becomes this snowball...one that feels like it will last forever, but one that *can't* last forever.

People start speculating on real estate. They put up buildings with no tenants in the hope that it will be filled. Still not at the top of the cycle, but it's close.

Now there's an oversupply—we almost always do this as supply and demand equal out. The curve, which had been steadily inclining, is now beginning to slide downward—and the downside of the curve is steeper.

It's as if banks and everyone else simply forgot the past. After twenty years you've got a lot of new people working at the bank. Some people won't even remember the last time it was hard. They don't scrutinize deals as tightly as they should. Nor do developers or deal sponsors—and we all pay for it.

When you suddenly get a slight oversupply in real estate, it's hard to fill a project—whether it's residential, office, or industrial. When that happens, there's no money coming in, which means there isn't enough money to pay the bank. Banks don't want to own real estate. They'll fire-sale and take their loss. Let's say that happens on a deal where the bank loaned $80 million. They now get only $50 million back. So now they have $30 million less in capital—except that it's worse for them than that, because it isn't just happening on one deal. It's how the cycle works. It's happening on deals everywhere. Their capital is drying up. AND banks loan out a multiple of their capital—like four to five times! So when they lose $30 million, they might have to get $120 million (or more) in loans off their books—scary!

That means they're suddenly not just handing loans out left and right anymore. They're focused on pulling in loans. As loans come due, borrowers have to pay off the balance or risk foreclosure. Cash is tight. No more building, bye-bye jobs, downsizing. Welcome to the downturn, where we started.

THE CURRENT OPPORTUNITY—AND RISKS

If you're reading this a long time after the publication of this book (2019), do some research and make your decisions based on where we are in the real estate cycle. But here's where we are right now.

As I'm writing this (2019), we are in a full-fledged development cycle. You can pretty much build anything anywhere right now, if it's in the right location. If you pick solid, well-thought-out projects, and if you can analyze supply and demand in a specific market, you can make money. But you can't find anything to buy right now. If you see there's a need for 5,000 homes in a given market and see there's only about 100 in the planning phase, go find some land and work with someone on a real estate deal who's thinking of putting in a residential community, because the chances are you'll do quite well on that. It is ALWAYS prudent to be very cautious in the development cycle.

The development cycle is not the time to be buying existing real estate assets. It's possible, but recognize that you'll pay more for the property, so the returns won't be quite as good. You'll have to rely on raising rents because that's the only way to get the returns you'll want. Most of these deals, though, don't pass the smell test: something is off about them. That's why it's time to develop.

Since we're in this phase of the cycle, nobody has been building in the last ten years, meaning there's no supply of existing real estate assets. Yet the population has been increasing, so there's demand for people to get into buildings and homes. You can get in on development deals, which have a shorter time frame, allowing you to get in and out of them quickly if need be. It's even possible to develop an apartment or office building that a REIT will buy at a premium after development.

For example, we recently saw that there was a demand for townhomes in Denver, but there weren't any on the market. So we built a bunch of townhomes, which took us about twenty months, and sold every one of them before construction was finished. Understanding market supply and demand is one way we can mitigate risk in these developments.

Development deals can be risky, though. You have to be careful. For example, one major risk with development deals is that things can take longer than you anticipated—in fact, you should expect them to take longer. Sometimes deals get stuck. There can be financing delays, permitting issues, labor issues, weather delays, and cost overruns, just to name a few. If we think it will take twenty-four months to turn around a project and get our investors' money back, we'll often say it'll take thirty months at least. Why? Because nobody ever complains about getting their money from a deal too early. Most people tend to over-promise and under-deliver, whether it's with returns, time frames, or the costs of construction. We try very hard to be conservative, especially on our time frames, but some things take longer than expected. It happens. Expect it.

As the investor, you could try to plan on those delays

while at the same time getting a feel for how well your deal sponsor projects things. For instance, if you were in the middle of building something in 2007, you'd probably still own it in 2015 because eight years passed where you couldn't do anything with that asset. If a deal is done correctly, your risk of losing your money is pretty low. You want to make sure you're buying (or building) things based on some predictable factors like supply and demand, rather than predicting the economy will fall off a cliff or rise sharply.

DOWNTURNS: OVERLOOKED OPPORTUNITIES

This development cycle can't last forever—it typically lasts five to seven years, maybe ten. It's tough to say. If you have the experience, you can see it coming. The economy tanked, and nobody could afford anything. People had to move back in with their parents, and the world came to an end, basically.

Oftentimes in a downturn, people see asset values go down and get scared. They wonder when it will happen again. The pain is still fresh in their minds. What they should be doing is picking up existing real estate because, as we saw in the explanation of the real estate cycle, it's so cheap in a downturn. Buy up assets while they're cheap and hold on to them indefinitely, because the market will almost certainly recover in time. You just have to be patient. And have plenty of cash on hand to pay down debt so that you can cash flow. Again, a great question for a deal sponsor is "What happens if things don't go as planned?"

Usually the recovery comes first to residential properties. Apartments are the first thing to come back. Then industrial, because people will still be buying things and making products. Then multi-tenant buildings (office spaces) tend to come back next, because slowly more people will need offices and companies can start expanding again. For about ten years from 2007 until 2016, nobody was building anything because banks wouldn't make loans. This is what created the opportunity to buy existing properties.

At that time, people might have said it was impossible to buy existing property because there was no capital available, but I knew there was opportunity there. If nobody can do something, and you can figure out how to do it (either by using investor capital or by having the balance sheet to be able to personally guarantee the debt), then you have an opportunity to make a lot of long-term passive income. If it's a good asset, you can buy and hold indefinitely.

When we were buying existing buildings from 2009 to 2012, people told us we were insane, especially in Michigan. They said, "Don't forget to turn the lights off when you're the last ones to leave the state." It was like pulling teeth to get people to invest with us. I had to call up my investors and say, "Now's the time. The exact reasons why you don't want to invest in a real estate deal right now are the same reasons you should be—because nobody else is."

LIVE A LITTLE

If you're seeing consistent money over time, my advice to people, believe it or not, is to get in the habit of spending some of it. I have very few investors I work with who actually spend any of their retirement dollars—they don't touch their principal. Obviously, this depends on your financial situation, but assuming you're an accredited investor (or an aspiring accredited investor), you'll have a high income and high net worth. You've probably gained a substantial part of your wealth because of your strict spending habits. I have little old ladies invested with me who have $10 million in the bank, but they don't know what to do with it—they're never going to find a way to spend it, and they don't have kids to give it to. I find myself in the weird position of telling them to go buy a flashy Cadillac, give some money to charity, or travel first class. They say, "I could never buy a new car or fly first class." I tell them they have to—they saved the money. But because of those spending habits, they don't want to.

My point is you need to live a little. Have some fun; go in style! Or help someone else get a roof over their head and a hot meal.

A short time ago, I had to call Delta and upgrade my parents on their way back from Johannesburg. A seventeen-hour overnight flight, and they had booked coach! That would be absolutely fine if they were on pace to outlive their money. It's an insane thing to do to yourself if you are seventy-five and don't even touch your nest egg because you can live off your Social Security checks.

CHAPTER FIVE

Investor Due Diligence

Now that you've identified a deal sponsor that you might be interested in working with, you need to figure out if they're good or not. This sounds easy in theory, but it's really not. As an investor, I can tell you that discerning who is legit and who isn't is not an innate ability. You have to know the right questions to ask. And asking the right questions might make you uncomfortable—you may feel like you're putting the deal sponsor on the spot or being too personal. However, as a deal sponsor, I can promise you that when investors ask me difficult questions, it's my favorite part of the process.

THE BASIC CRITERIA FOR IDENTIFYING THE RIGHT DEAL SPONSOR

You've identified some potential deal sponsors, so now you need to get on the phone—or better, meet face-to-face—and ask those tough questions. Some organizations might not have the time to sit down with you, preferring to send you a packet in the mail or by email. That's fine. They should still be able to answer your questions in one form or another, even if you can communicate only via phone or email. Here are the criteria you need to identify.

MOTIVATION

You don't need to be a human lie detector, but if you sit down for a conversation with a potential deal sponsor and ask questions, you'll be able to gauge whether or not they are a genuinely honest person based on their answers. When people ask me why I invest in real estate, I say that for one, it's fun for me. My motto is this: have fun, help people, learn something, and make some money along the way (in that order too).

Of course, wanting money is part of it—about twenty years ago, when I started out in real estate, I needed money, so that became one of my primary motivations, just behind learning. In time I was able to build an effective business, gaining money and experience, and money became less important. The money component is still there—I don't make deals unless they make money—but if something isn't fun for me, I don't have to do it. What's fun for me now is helping people and having fun. I get a real kick out of being able to use all the knowledge I've acquired to make an on-the-spot decision about a multimillion-dollar deal. I love making deals. So when people ask me my motivation, I'm very transparent. I tell them I'm in it to make money, but I'm in it because I love deals and I love helping other people make money. Your deal sponsors should be that transparent too. You should be able to determine if their motivation is to make themselves money, or if they're deeply motivated to make other people money.

What to ask?

Ask them why (other than making money) they do this. Why this job of all jobs and not something else? Why did they choose real estate instead of being a doctor or an engineer? What gets them out of bed every day?

Also, ask what their motivation is for putting a deal together. What do they look for? What's driving them to do this particular deal?

Lastly, just talk to them about their life, and listen. Find their story of why they do what they do—in real estate and elsewhere.

PASSION

Ensure that the deal sponsor has a passion for real estate investing. This is different than motivation in that we're all motivated by different things—someone might be driven to make money but lack the passion for real estate. Maybe it was just the business they fell into or inherited. I sometimes joke that I'm a deal junkie. Like I said earlier, I just love to make deals. It's the kind of thing I'd want to do, money or no money. Passion is a result of having fun, and the true professionals will find ways to have fun with the process.

This is important because development can be very, very challenging and, at times, not fun at all. That's especially true if you are someone who avoids challenging situations and has trouble taking a tough situation and looking at it as an opportunity for personal growth.

You want someone who's not just up to the challenge, but who will attack that challenge. This isn't just about *whether* or not they'll get tough, but *why* they will stay engaged when the going gets tough. Why do they endeavor to take on whatever it is they are presenting, representing, to you?

What to ask?

Ask them about a deal that got tough and how they dealt with it. Ask them about some of their toughest challenges.

If that feels too direct—or at least something you might want to build up to—ask them, more generally speaking, what kinds of things could go wrong with a deal. Then it's easy to ask them if they've ever dealt with any of those. Just be curious. Ask for the story. If they're being vague or evasive, it might be time to look elsewhere. If they get excited and give you all the details from the battlefield, you're probably in good hands.

INTEGRITY

Is the deal sponsor going to do what's best for everyone involved, or are they going to do what's best for themselves? In an ideal world, those two goals will be aligned. For me, integrity means reporting not only the things that are going right but also the things that aren't going according to plan. Likewise, it means spelling out to the investors (that's you) how they're going to fix those things that aren't going right.

If something requires that I step in to fix it, I'm going to do it, and so should your deal sponsor. Last week I was up at a northern Michigan lake doing nothing. I'm not a seventy-hour-a-week kind of guy, and my investors know that about me because I'm honest and upfront. But they also know that I'm the guy who will leave the lake and take care of anything that could go wrong with a deal.

You should always feel like you know the things you need

to know. At all initial investor meetings and/or phone conversations, I clearly explain that there will likely be bumps in the road. They likely won't hear about many of them because we tend to solve them without any significant change to the deal. BUT I explain that the team behind the deal is more important than the deal itself, and that I am very open to answering any and all questions they have about our past deals, our team, and our track record.

Look for sponsors who VOLUNTEER this information and openness.

What to ask?

Ask them if they have any reports from past deals you could look at. Ask for an initial investment packet from a previous deal, and every update and report on that deal and a final conclusion of that deal. That way you can look at a case study. Look to see if they were consistent and honest during the whole transaction.

Also ask them to volunteer some information. Every deal sponsor has hit bumps in the road. They should have a story or two. Ask them, "Can you describe a time when you admitted a mistake on one of your deals? Can you share a time with me when you've had to give investors bad news? What have you done to earn the trust of your investors?"

KNOWLEDGE

Knowledge is critical to the process. Reading, writing, and giving talks about real estate and investing are all great things to do, but my knowledge of the industry isn't driven home unless I'm actively participating in deals. I learn through experience.

You can ask one simple question to gauge a deal sponsor's knowledge level: "While I've got you on the phone, what books can you recommend for me to learn more about real estate and real estate investing?"

They should have an answer. Maybe it will be one of the books in the next paragraph. But if they don't have an answer, then you're likely dealing with someone who doesn't spend their time learning about the thing that you're about to put a lot of money into. That can be a problem.

Or maybe you'd ask them specifically what they thought of Robert T. Kiyosaki's *Rich Dad, Poor Dad* series, or Samuel K. Freshman's *Principles of Real Estate Syndication*, or even Carleton Sheets's *No Down Payment* program. You might even throw out a Warren Buffett biography, just for good measure. Your deal sponsor should be well-read and current on what's going on in the real estate world. If they haven't read specific books you mention, ask them where they got, and continue to get, their knowledge.

Ask, "Where did you take classes? Do you have a Certified Commercial Investment Member (CCIM) designation? Where did you learn to do what you do here? Who mentored you?"

Again, they should have an answer—or several. If they don't, get back to prospecting.

EXPERIENCE

Find out how long your potential sponsor has been in the real estate investing industry. Ask, "What are some of your better deals? What has been your worst deal?" This is similar to some of the earlier questions about integrity, but you also want to get a feel for how familiar they are with the landscape. Do they sound like someone who has experience, or like someone who is winging it a bit?

With age comes experience. This is important: when it comes to real estate, age isn't just a number. At twenty-eight, I took on my first investors—my parents. I don't recommend choosing your son as a deal sponsor, but they took a risk and cosigned on a loan for me because it was the only way I could buy a portfolio of houses that I had found and put under contract for purchase. They made a lot of money on that deal in the end. However, except in extraordinary situations, a deal sponsor should be in their late thirties or older and have completed hundreds of real estate transactions, because experience is the only way to learn real estate investing.

This creates another chicken-and-egg problem for the sponsor. BUT it's not YOUR PROBLEM! So don't make it your problem—keep looking for the right deal sponsor. How do sponsors get experience if they don't have investors? For me, it came with doing small deals over a long period of time with my own money.

Remember, it's not just about age. Just because a person is fifty doesn't mean they are qualified. If, for example, they just quit their job as a doctor to become a real estate entrepreneur, then they are not qualified. So age is just one thing to take into consideration. Over time, experienced deal sponsors have learned how to spot potential pitfalls and know how to deal with them. Less experienced sponsors don't have this advantage. An overnight success usually takes twenty-plus years.

It's okay if they are younger and starting out (that was me once), but just know that your money may become their education.

CHECK THEIR REPUTATION

Experience breeds a good reputation.

As a person working in real estate, the deal sponsor will inevitably do work with banks and accounting firms—reputable institutions that you can verify information with. Ask the sponsor who they borrow money from and if you can get in touch with their contacts at the bank. This may be a level of due diligence that only a few people go into, but it pays off, trust me—especially if you're skeptical. If you're coming from California, for example, and you're investing with a guy from Michigan, you might not have any connections with him. You could get a great feeling from him over the phone, but you're just a tad paranoid that you're being taken in by a Ponzi scheme or something similar. That's when you ask to talk to their contact at their bank. I can empathize with that point of view, since I'm always looking for how I'm going to get screwed on a deal. Having a healthy skeptic in you is a good thing as long as you don't let it paralyze you from doing anything.

You can also ask to talk to people they've worked with for a while. They should be willing to give you references. Find out what their investors think about them. If you do a Google search for my company, Promanas, you'll find articles about us on MLive.com and in other places, which tells you our reputation is good. You should be able to find that kind of information on any deal sponsors who have any kind of experience.

Get a few names of people who have been in a deal with

the sponsor from start to finish. Were the initial projections represented met? Exceeded? I've asked this question of hundreds of my investors about other investments they've participated in, and I've found ALMOST NONE that have worked out. Yes, in some cases they've made some money, but NOT what was originally projected. Over-promise, under-deliver seems to be the norm in this industry. I know why this happens, and it's not normally done on purpose. A deal sponsor is putting out the best numbers they can justify—this is a terrible approach, but they want to attract the money, so they do what they have to.

Therefore, a KEY QUESTION FOR THEM should be this: "What are the contingency fees in this deal? What are the layers of protection, or reserves, or other items that can be cut out in case of lower rents or sale prices and/or higher-than-projected costs?" Write that one down—that question is worth the price of admission, and it applies to more than just a real estate deal.

GENEROSITY

I like people who are generous with their time and knowledge. How long is this deal sponsor willing to spend with you? The answer to this question will be a good indicator of their generosity. Coming right out and asking them if they're generous might be a weird question no matter how you ask it, so this is more of a judgment call.

Ask yourself some questions here: Are they being generous with their time? Are they willing to share their time and answer your questions? Or do you feel that they are rushed and/or annoyed with you?

Of course, you want to be respectful of their time, but it's important to know that the best deal sponsors will want to share knowledge with people who are genuinely curious. Their religious, political, and other beliefs DO NOT need to line up with yours (unless that's important to you, but it will limit your circle if you stick to Buddhists only or far-right Republicans or any other smaller category of people). If they're being honest and open and generous with their time, then that's what counts. We are getting large enough that I can't possibly spend the kind of time with my investors that I used to. That was one of the main motivators for this book, and for building an investor relations department.

TRANSPARENCY

Similar to generosity, this is something you'll feel out as you ask your other questions—and you better. Transparency is the first and most important thing to look for in a deal sponsor. A lot of people don't like to volunteer their information because they think a 100-page packet, for example, would create paralysis by analysis in their investors. But if you're asking for it, they should be willing to give it.

You don't have to understand every detailed explanation and subcategory in the records the sponsor provides. The fact that they're open to full disclosure is what's important here. Even if you don't review the records, their willingness to provide them speaks volumes.

Transparency doesn't mean they divulge personal details to the point where they're spilling the beans about the first person they ever kissed—that's not what I mean by transparency. What I mean is if you want to look at their records, such as a specific appraisal or closing statement, or even references of bank contacts, all of that should be fair game. A good deal sponsor will be open and willing to provide that information.

Your deal sponsor should be willing to give you any and all information you want to see. If you ask them to share profit and loss statements for their current or previous deals and they say no, or you feel like they're avoiding you, that's a red flag. Same thing if you get vague answers when you ask how their previous deals are doing now. Find out what they report to their current members about those deals. We'll talk a little more about that later, but for now, if it's not much or nothing: red flag. Good reporting is critical. Remember, this is supposed to be a *passive* activity for you. Chasing around a deal sponsor for updates isn't passive—it's frustrating.

Another potential question to ask a deal sponsor is how they fared between 2007 and 2010. A lot of people, including the true professionals, ran into trouble during that time frame. That doesn't make them bad at their job, but it does mean they should have learned a lot. They should have a story and should be able to answer you. You could learn a lot about how transparent they are. Are they dodging the question or being straightforward? What measures have they taken since? Do they blame the market, or do they take responsibility for whatever went wrong? (If they weren't in business at the time, then you're still learning something: they haven't been doing this long.)

No deal sponsor has hit a home run on every deal they've done. A transparent sponsor should be willing to share the results of all of the deals they've done regardless of how successful they were.

TEAM

Ask the deal sponsor, "How many people are in your office? Who are they? What is their background? What do they do?" You want to understand if everyone in their company has the same motivations they have. It doesn't take a huge team to run deals, but everyone needs a top CPA/CFO, a director of operations, and some administrative staff. This is an enormous chicken-and-egg problem. For the first deals I did, it was just me and a personal assistant—that was it. But I had a solid (outsourced) team of professionals assembled. I could give investors assurances that I could handle it because I had a CPA and a top legal firm, as well as others who comprised my team even though they didn't work full time with me. I made it happen, and so should your deal sponsor.

FINANCIAL STRENGTH

I wouldn't necessarily expect a deal sponsor to send you their financial statements, but they should be able to give you an idea of their financial strength. By definition, if the loan they're getting or the deals you're considering require a personal guarantee and the deal sponsor is the guarantor of those loans, then the bank has verified their financial strength. In that case, you won't need to verify anything.

Let me give an example. I'm in a deal to build a $40 million hotel in Denver—my investors and I put in about $13 million, and we've got a loan for the other $27 million. You can figure that my financial strength is good if I'm the only guarantor on the loan. If I'm calling you, the investor, and I'm asking you to be on the loan with me, that should throw up some huge red flags. *Never invest in a deal where you're asked to be a guarantor on the loan. Never.*

I'm also very wary of deals where the sponsor doesn't have to guarantee the loan. That's called non-recourse financing. We've talked about this previously; it means they can simply walk away and turn in the keys to the property if the deal doesn't work out (not good for you). Recourse loans are like handcuffs; so is a great reputation and a strong presence in the community.

Experience, transparency, knowledge, motivation, passion, and integrity: they are all important in finding the right deal sponsor. The good news is you can always take your money and put it elsewhere if the first person doesn't work out, but doing your due diligence is critical, both in terms of the sponsor and the deal itself.

GETTING PERSONAL

A good deal sponsor should be open and candid about their business (as well as some personal) background. They should be forthcoming about their familial status, how long they've been in their community, their educational background, and even their charitable interests.

Don't be shy or afraid to ask any questions. Have a conversation. Let things come up.

The best question I've ever been asked is, "What's the worst deal you ever did and what did you learn from it?"

You can learn a lot about a sponsor with that question. People love the big company or the big deal, but the smaller guy will be more willing to give you a personal touch, such as an interview.

SKIN IN THE GAME

It's critical to find out if your sponsor invests in their own deals. It may be the case that a sponsor doesn't have any money readily available to get into a specific deal. That happens. When I was starting out, I didn't have any money of my own; it was all tied up in the single-family home portfolio I'd built. What I did inform people of, though, was that I was putting my parents' money or my close friends' money in our deals—and their money is more important than my own (transparency). I had skin in the game in the form of personal guarantees with the bank and in the form of my family and friends' money. Now that my older deals are liquidating, I can put my own cash into deals and buy shares just like my investors do.

PUT YOUR MONEY WHERE YOUR MOUTH IS

The private placement memorandum will spell out that the SEC hasn't reviewed the investment, meaning only accredited investors can put money in. The PPM also details the exact nature of the sponsor's involvement in the deal, along with potential conflicts of interest. Even given these standard inclusions in a PPM, you should have some good questions on the tip of your tongue for when you're talking to a deal sponsor. If you can't understand what they're talking about, then don't do the deal. It's that simple.

If somebody can't explain to you in layman's terms what's in the PPM, then they don't understand it well enough themselves. It's my responsibility as the deal sponsor to make you money. If I don't, then guess who comes after me? It's not just Mr. and Mrs. Investor; it's the bank, because I personally guarantee loans for many of the deals I put together.

A lot of people can put together what we call a non-recourse deal. It's pretty rare that we do these types of deals. Most of our deals require that somebody signs a personal guarantee, and that somebody is me. The personal guarantee allows a set of checks and balances that I don't mind having because it's putting our money where our mouth is.

That's the most important indicator to look for when investing in somebody's deal: who's guaranteeing the debts of the company? If the sponsor can walk away from a deal when times get tough, without obligation to pay back the bank, that should be a red flag. Look, things are going to come up. What's the glue that is going to hold that sponsor to the deal? Maybe it's not the type of loan, but then what is it? Ask, "If things don't go as planned, why are you going to show up and do your best to the very end?" All you can really be sure of is that you will get someone's best efforts—that should be inherent in the deal structure or situation.

Chapter Six

Accredited Investors and Smart Investors

Let's get one thing straight, or sort of straight. You can be an accredited investor but NOT a smart investor. You can be a smart investor but NOT be accredited. You can also be a smart investor who is accredited as well. Let me try to clarify a few things.

If you don't meet the criteria discussed in Chapter Three, then I'm forced to remind you that you can't participate in these types of deals. But before you get too discouraged, let's talk offering memorandum (OM) and private placement memorandum (PPM) for a minute. Investopedia says (and I'm paraphrasing a bit):

An offering memorandum (OM) is a legal document that

states the objectives, risks and terms of an investment involved with a private placement. It is a very abbreviated version of the whole deal—all the basics you'd want to know without all the nitty gritty details you'd only want to know if you were interested in the deal. And that's the whole point of an offering memorandum—it's a document you use to see if it's a deal you might be interested it. It includes items such as a company's financial statements, management biographies, a detailed description of the business operations and more. An offering memorandum (sometimes called a deal deck) serves to provide buyers with information on the offering and to protect the sellers from the liability associated with selling unregistered securities. It's like a teaser. And if the deal looks good, then we get into the details with a private placement memorandum (PPM).

A PPM is a document that spells out and discloses everything that the deal sponsor knows about the deal. It's designed to PROTECT the person creating the deal. A good sponsor will disclose EVERYTHING they can (that's one of the signs of a good sponsor). The idea here is that if you, the investor, lose all your money and try to come after the sponsor, that sponsor can point to this document and say, "It says you can lose all your money."

It's very important that you read the PPM because the sponsor SHOULD spell out the deal in great detail. If you don't understand it but you feel the sponsor is honest and good, have them walk you through it on the phone or in person. If they are too busy, they should have an investor relations person who can do this. If you can't get questions answered, steer clear. This is far from rocket science. A smart investor invests in what they can understand.

There are dueling beliefs as to why these laws came into being. On the one hand, if you're an accredited investor, you have money and can afford to take risks, so the regulations help protect unsophisticated investors. However, others also believe that the laws were created in order to make sure PPM opportunities went only to country club members. The rich get richer.

Whatever the reason for their existence, private placement deals are like the Wild West of investing. There are advantages, but also risks, that come with them. Once you meet the criteria to enter the Wild West, you're free to make deals in an unregulated industry.

Once someone files with the SEC, they can pretty much do whatever they want. This Wild West environment allows people with no track records to put a PPM together and yet have no net worth of their own to back the deal.

If someone gets information on a deal that we are doing, we send them a questionnaire that they have to fill out and they need someone else to verify it. It looks like this:

PF4, LLC

c/o James A. Schriemer, Conlin, McKenney & Philbrick, P.C.
350 South Main Street, Suite 400, Ann Arbor, MI 48104

Ladies and Gentlemen:

The following information is submitted to you in connection with my proposed purchase of a membership interest offered by PF4, LLC. It is my understanding the information will be held by Conlin, McKenney & Philbrick, counsel for the company, and will be treated as confidential and disclosed only as they deem appropriate in connection with establishing the offering of such membership interests as exempt from registration under the Securities Act of 1933, the Michigan Uniform Securities Act (and/or other applicable state laws), or disclosed as otherwise required by law.

INSTRUCTIONS

The sections of this Questionnaire must be completed as follows:

SECTION A	All Purchasers
SECTION B	Only Purchasers who are corporations, limited liability companies, trusts or partnerships
SECTION C	All Individual Purchasers (except Purchasers meeting the requirements of Section B(6))
SIGNATURE PAGE	All Purchasers

SECTION A

GENERAL INFORMATION
ALL PURCHASERS MUST COMPLETE

1. Please print the exact name of the individual(s) or entity who will own:_____

_____

Type of Ownership (check one):

_____	Individual	_____	Corporation
_____	Joint tenants with rights of survivorship	_____	Partnership
_____	Revocable Grantor Trust	_____	Limited Liability Company
_____	Irrevocable Trust		

3. Please furnish the following information for each investor or beneficiary of a grantor trust (as applicable):

Investor 1	Investor 2 (for joint investors only)
Name: _____	Name: _____
Residence/Principal Office Address: _____	Residence/Principal Office Address:_____
Date of Birth: _____	Date of Birth: _____
Marital Status: _____	Marital Status: _____
SS# or EIN#: _____	SS# or EIN#: _____
State of Primary Residence: _____	State of Primary Residence: _____
State Where You Vote: _____	State Where You Vote: _____
State Where You Maintain Your Driver's License: _____	State Where You Maintain Your Driver's License: _____
Telephone Number: _____	Telephone Number: _____
Email Address: _____	Email Address: _____

SECTION B

ACCREDITED INVESTORS ACKNOWLEDGMENT
(ONLY FOR CORPORATIONS, PARTNERSHIPS, TRUSTS, AND LIMITED LIABILITY COMPANIES)

Accredited partnership, corporation, limited liability companies or revocable grantor trust entities must initial at least one of the following statements. Revocable grantor trust entities with total assets of $5,000,000 or less should initial statement (1) and complete Section C with respect to the grantor. Other accredited trust entities should initial one of the following statements other than (1).

An individual is an "accredited investor" if the individual has personal income (excluding income attributable to a spouse) of more than $200,000 or joint income with that person's spouse in excess of $300,000 in each of the two most recent years, and has a reasonable expectation of reaching the same income level in the current year, or has an individual net worth (either individually or jointly with a spouse) in excess of $1 million, excluding the equity value of and mortgage debt related to the investor's principal residence.

_____ (1) The investor hereby certifies that all of the equity owners of the investor are accredited investors as defined above or in one of the statements in (2) through (9) below of this Section B (each equity owner of the investor must complete a separate Section C of this Questionnaire). The following is a list of all the equity investors:

1) _____   3) _____
2) _____   4) _____

_____ (2) The investor hereby certifies that it is a bank as defined in Section 3(a)(2) of the Act, whether acting in its individual or fiduciary capacity.

_____ (3) The investor hereby certifies that it is an insurance company as defined in Section 2(13) of the Act.

_____ (4) The investor hereby certifies that it is an investment company registered under the Investment Company Act of 1940, or a business development company as defined in Section 2(a)(48) of that Act.

_____ (5) The investor hereby certifies that it is a Small Business Investment Company licensed by the U.S. Small Business Administration under Section 301(c) or (d) of the Small Business Investment Act of 1958.

_____ (6) The investor hereby certifies that it is an employee benefit plan within the meaning of Title I of the Employee Retirement Income Security Act of 1974, and its investment decision is being made by a plan fiduciary, as defined in Section 3(21) of that Act, which is either a bank, insurance company, or registered investment adviser, or the employee benefit plan has total assets in excess of $5,000,000.

_____ (7) The investor hereby certifies that it is a private business development company as defined in Section 202(a)(22) of the Investment Advisers Act of 1940.

_____ (8) The investor hereby certifies that it is a non-profit organization described in Section 501(c)(3) of the Internal Revenue Code, with total assets in excess of $5,000,000.

_____ (9) Any trust, corporation, limited liability company or partnership with total assets in excess of $5,000,000, not formed for the specific purpose of acquiring the securities offered, whose purchase is directed by a person who has such knowledge and experience in financial and business matters and is capable of valuing the merits and risks of the investment.

SECTION C

FINANCIAL INFORMATION
ALL INDIVIDUAL INVESTORS MUST COMPLETE
(Please check the appropriate response.)

1. Individual income, **excluding** income of spouse, for 2016:
   _____ $200,000 or less   ____ more than $200,000

2. Individual income, **excluding** income of spouse, for 2017:
   _____ $200,000 or less   ____ more than $200,000

3. Estimated individual income, **excluding** income of spouse, for 2018:
   _____ $200,000 or less   ____ more than $200,000

4. Individual income joint **with** spouse for 2016:
   _____ $300,000 or less   ____ more than $300,000

5. Individual income joint **with** spouse for 2017:
   _____ $300,000 or less   ____ more than $300,000

6. Estimated individual income joint **with** spouse for 2018:
   _____ $300,000 or less   ____ more than $300,000

7. Net worth*, individually, or jointly with your spouse:
   _____ $999,999 or less   ____ $1,000,000 or more

* **In determining net worth, the equity value of and mortgage debt related to the investor's principal residence should be excluded.**

SIGNATURE PAGE

ALL INVESTORS MUST COMPLETE

IN WITNESS WHEREOF, the undersigned purchaser(s) has completed and executed this Questionnaire this day of _____, 2018.

INDIVIDUALS:

_____   _____
Signature of Purchaser 1   Signature of Purchaser 2

_____   _____
Print Name of Purchaser 1   Print Name of Purchaser 2

ENTITIES: (Corporations, Trusts, Partnerships and Limited Liability Companies)

Entity Name: _____

By: _____
                    (Signature)

_____
                    (Print Name)

Its: _____
                    (Title)

PLEASE NOTE: **You must also provide PF4, LLC with an Accredited Investor Verification Form completed by your accountant, attorney, investment advisor or broker-dealer.**

The deal sponsor (us) does not verify this information. The SEC does not verify this information. I have no idea who would ever check on this information, but we are required to get this form. My best guess is that if a deal went bad, then all sorts of rocks would get turned over and an SEC agent would ask for this information on every one of our investors. They would want to make sure that we (again, the sponsor) were not taking advantage of unsophisticated investors or unqualified investors.

You often hear about the deals that don't work (Bernie Madoff, anybody?). Every once in a while, you'll read about somebody who put together $20 million from little old ladies in a retirement community somewhere, then kept the money and ran off. These scams do happen, but they're the exception, not the rule. Most often, the bad deals are due to a lack of experience from the person putting them together—a sponsor who does not properly quantify the risks.

Although you need to be an accredited investor for most private offerings, anyone can invest in publicly traded real estate offerings, such as real estate investment trusts (or REITs). Some are private, non-traded REITs, and others are publicly traded REITs. For publicly traded REITs, anyone can buy in and sell out because the company has gone through a layer of scrutiny that requires them to file forms with the SEC every quarter. These public

REITs have to disclose everything—it's a very rigorous and expensive process.

So while the Wild West environment of PPMs comes with certain risks, it also comes with potential rewards you won't find in REITs. With fewer regulations, the returns can be that much greater. One of the advantages of the PPM is that you avoid the burden and expense and paperwork that come with SEC filings required by a REIT, as well as hefty brokerage expenses. Your company can add those saved expenses to the bottom line and make everyone more money. Everyone appreciates that.

You don't necessarily need to be an accredited investor to put money in real estate. You can still buy a house, fix it up, and sell it, or purchase a two-bedroom condo and rent it out. You only have to meet the accredited investor criteria to invest in PPM deals like the ones we put together. These PPM deals are designed for passive investors (we'll discuss the different kinds of deals and their risk levels in the next chapter). If you want to invest in real estate but don't want to spend your time fixing toilets and dealing with tenants, then passive investing is for you.

PATIENT INVESTORS ARE SMART INVESTORS

Just because you're an accredited investor doesn't mean you're a smart investor. We have hundreds of accredited investors who participate in our deals at Promanas. Some of them I would describe as very, very smart investors. Others only meet the accredited investor criteria and are, frankly, lucky to have found a deal through us—I see them invest in other things outside of our deals that I wouldn't necessarily describe as "smart."

Smart investors are patient. They understand the long-term nature of investing in general. They know that they can't chase yields or try to double their money overnight. Real estate investing isn't about getting rich quick; it's about getting rich slowly, consistently, and faithfully—it's a buy-and-hold investment. Once a smart investor finds the right person to invest with, they're more willing to be passive. They might have questions, of course—a lot of our investors have very good questions, which we like to answer—but on some level, most of our investors flip a mental switch where they say, "I trust this guy. He's been making me money for a long time." You sit back, let the deal sponsor make you money, and ask if there's any way you can help—that's what a smart investor does.

PASSIVE INVESTING IS SMART INVESTING

Passive investing lets you take the emotion and time out of your investments. When you buy Google stock, you don't call the company up and tell them how to run their business like an armchair quarterback. You sit back and let the stock rise. If you look at robo-advisors like Wealthfront, they use math rather than emotion to move money around in index funds—they want to take themselves out of the equation. Investors say to themselves, "As a human being, I know I'm an emotional creature. My stockbroker thinks he can do better than the S&P 500, but statistically speaking, that's highly improbable, so I'm just going to buy an S&P 500 index fund."

You may be wondering, "Why passive? Shouldn't smart investors educate themselves about real estate law and economics?" On the contrary, smart investors don't get bogged down in real estate details. They focus on finding the right partner. I've asked all the smartest people I've ever met with (including directors of investments for major billion-dollar endowment funds) what they focus on most when they're considering investing in a private real estate deal. Almost all of them focus primarily on the person putting the deal together. Of course, these smart investors look at the deal itself and get a feel for its chances of success, but more importantly, they look at the sponsor's track record. They run background checks. They look at their history. They ask lots of questions. The smartest people I've ever met with spend more time asking questions about me than they do about the specific deal. "What's my downside?" the smart investors ask. "I'm not so concerned with doubling my money overnight;

I'm concerned about *losing* my money." In other words, they take a "protection of wealth" strategy.

DR. DEAL SPONSOR

Think of smart investing as being similar to visiting the doctor. Like most people, I don't just call up the first doctor I find in the phone book; I do a little research. I know people—I get recommendations from my social circle. I call one doctor and see what he has to say before making an appointment. The problem is that many times patients think they know everything. They've searched online for symptoms and they're arrogant, so they disregard the doctor's advice. The same thing happens with investors: the more they think they know about real estate, the less they actually know. The curious investors are always the smart investors. When you find someone who clearly knows your issue and has seen hundreds of similar cases, you should follow their advice and continue working with them long-term.

Doctors have to go to medical school and maintain certain grades for a long time to become doctors. When a doctor gets out of medical school, they become a resident, where they're trained under another physician for a number of years specific to their field. In other words, there is a substantial weeding-out process in becoming a physician. Odds are you're not going to get a total nutjob doctor. In the private placement world, on the other hand, there exists no such school or weed-out process. That's why it becomes more important to ask questions of your deal sponsor.

Bottom line: smart investors will spend more time figuring out how the deal sponsor operates than on the details of the specific deal. They ask about the track records and performance. Likewise, a good sponsor will ask a lot of questions of the investor. Sponsors don't want to put someone in a deal where the investor expects to get out within three years when that deal is supposed to last ten, or vice versa. We ask lots of questions of our investors: "How old are you? How much money do you make? Are you looking to fund your retirement?" These can be uncomfortable, difficult conversations, but the smart investors and sponsors have no problem asking and answering difficult questions.

Here's another analogy: your deal sponsor should be like a good football coach—someone you can trust and who knows how to win.

Think of a college football team. The coach is an indicator of success more often than the team itself. Even if a team has great players, with a rotten coach those players run amok, aren't prepared, and lose games. You have to look at the coach's track record to find out if he's good or not:

"How many games has he won? How many has he lost? What programs has he coached for? Has he had enough time to build the program?"

My point is that with the same players and a different coach, a bad team becomes a good team, and vice versa. The same thing is true of an investment deal. Good deal, bad deal, it doesn't matter. Issues and challenges pop up as the deal progresses, and they can be handled poorly by the wrong deal sponsor, or they can be handled well.

SMART DOESN'T MEAN SEXY

The smart investors who invest with us are doing it because of our team and our track record. We don't sell deals. We sell our team and our track record. Most of our business is a direct referral from an existing investor. They call in and we put them on our potential investor list. Any time we have a deal, we'll send it out to our entire list. We might reach out to someone and nudge them along if we think it's a good deal for them specifically, but sometimes people just don't have the cash or it's not the right time. Other times we see people on our list who never invest. We'll ask them about it and they'll say they'd like to get their house paid off first before investing. Fair enough. But then we see them putting money in some "sexier" deal than the boring real estate deals we offer. Sexy deals are the deals that are exciting and sound like fun, but they are ultimately less profitable, or worse.

You see it all the time with restaurants. People will say, "I've always wanted to be part-owner of a restaurant." I'll say, "Great, invest $50,000 and wave goodbye to it. Then you can say you own part of that restaurant that may or may not be there in three years." Of course, there are some great restaurant owners I know who have done quite well, particularly around Ann Arbor. The deal itself isn't the difference-maker. Hard work and knowledge through years of experience are. The very best places I eat have an owner/operator who lives and breathes the business—daily.

Instead of owning a restaurant, how about owning the building in a great downtown location that a restaurant leases from you? Connect the dots. I don't ever want any business to fail, but if they do, another tenant will come along and pay to be there—and I'll keep making money.

DON'T LET ONE BAD DEAL SPOIL THE BUNCH

Another phenomenon I encounter with potential investors: they've previously invested in a private placement, maybe years ago, that didn't work out for them. They lost money on the deal and decided to never do it again. This is a mistake, in my opinion. In real estate investing, I like to say, "You either make a lot of money, or you learn a lot." Oftentimes, when you make a lot of money, you think you're a genius, but the reality is you didn't really learn anything. When you lose money, though, it wakes you up—you actually pay attention. That's when you really learn something.

When I started out, I invested in somebody else's private placements. I lost a substantial amount of money in some of those deals. I went back and reviewed them, and I realized that if I had read everything thoroughly, and if I had really evaluated the deal sponsor, I could have avoided those mistakes. I hadn't asked the right questions. I didn't even know *how* to ask the right questions. It wasn't that the sponsor was corrupt; it was that the market changed, things started going south, and he moved on—literally, moved out of state.

Now when I meet people who tell me they lost on a real estate investment deal, I dig a little deeper. I peel back the layers of the investment onion and find out that their particular deal never had a chance. When I point it out to them, I tell them they've gained serious knowledge: "If I were in your shoes, Mr. Smart Investor or Mr. Not-So-Smart Investor, if you are ever willing to do this again, I would take that knowledge and apply those lessons to the next deal."

Don't make the same mistake twice. That's how real wealth is built: by learning from your poor decisions and moving on.

You can be an accredited investor and not a smart one. Or you can be a smart investor and not necessarily meet the accredited investor criteria. Your goal should be both. Then find yourself a reputable deal sponsor, and move forward with some boring, profitable deals.

CHAPTER SEVEN

Types of Real Estate Investments

I've told you why you should invest in real estate and the necessity of being a smart, accredited investor by working with a deal sponsor. Now it's time to chat about the types of real estate investments available. This can get a little technical, but by this point you should have a solid handle on how to approach investing, and since you've made the smart choice to go with PPMs, it's important to understand what makes them special and where they fit into the larger investing world.

LEARNING FROM DIRECT INVESTING

You'll remember from Chapter Four that a common way many people get their toes wet is with direct real estate investments—that is, buying a property on their own without a deal sponsor. It's not automatically a horrible idea. There is money to be made. In fact, that's how I got my start. As a licensed real estate broker selling single-family homes in the early 1990s, I started finding properties that I thought made sense for me to purchase.

One of the first units I bought was a $50,000 two-bedroom condo. I put $5,000 down and borrowed the other $45,000 from the bank (I don't think you can still do that today). I found a friend to rent the second bedroom from me, which basically paid the mortgage and association fees. At that point, I needed to pay for utilities only. His rent was cheaper than he would've gotten elsewhere, and he covered a large portion of my living expenses—a true win-win for both of us. A year later, I sold the unit for $65,000, bought a bigger unit, and repeated my direct investment recipe. By the time I was in my late twenties, I had accumulated twenty single-family homes, looked after by a property manager and maintenance man I'd hired. I kept moving on to bigger and bigger deals.

So again, there's money to be made. But what I really gained during all that time was even more valuable: knowledge.

I didn't start talking to any investors until I had done every type of real estate transaction I could do on my own. My experience as a real estate broker was invaluable for my investing career. I think anyone interested in being a deal sponsor should really go through the trenches of earning a living as a real estate broker first, as that's where you help people find good deals and can gain tremendous experience on someone else's dime.

After about ten years I decided it was time to burn the ships, stop doing brokerage business, and start focusing 100 percent on crafting deals that could help others make money alongside me. I had learned a lot as a residential and commercial broker.

One deal in particular stands out in my memory. A client wanted to sell a piece of land not too far from where I live. I went to look at the lot and wondered what could go there. *What was it zoned for? What purpose would it serve?* I contacted the township and got a list of permitted uses for this land. A typical real estate broker will just put out a sign and hope it sells. I figured out what could go on the lot and made a sign that said, "PUT YOUR FAST FOOD FRANCHISE HERE." Lo and behold, a Steak 'n Shake came along and put the property under contract.

There is no substitute for real-world experience, but the important point here, and the whole point of this book, is that *you don't have to go and learn all that the hard way.*

That's because people like me, deal sponsors, have done it all for you. Find the right sponsor, and a lot of the real estate investment blood, sweat, and tears have been shed for you.

THE TIME SUCK OF DIRECT REAL ESTATE INVESTMENT

Before moving forward, let's talk a bit more about the pitfalls of direct real estate investment. I wouldn't just take my word that it's tough and probably not worth your time, especially if you're accredited. Let me share some of the knowledge I gained along the way.

I learned a lot through direct real estate investing, and perhaps more than anything, I learned it takes time. For example, in the deal mentioned earlier, wanting to make sure I saw things all the way through, I didn't just sit around with the purchase agreement in hand and wait for the deal to close. I went to all the meetings with the township. I watched Steak 'n Shake go through the approval process and the closing process. I saw how it all went down, and by doing so I made the most out of the learning experience of being a broker. I still remember all the tiny details we had to go through, like when the township made Steak 'n Shake change from wood chips to lava rocks outside the drive-through window because they were concerned that folks would be flicking their lit cigarettes out the window as they approached the drive-through. The approval process is one of the biggest deterrents on the planet to new development. To call it a "pain in the ass" is a massive understatement.

It's a great way to learn, in other words, and it's something you can do. But I say you're better off working with a deal sponsor who's already put in that time and has that knowledge and experience behind them.

ACTIVE VS. PASSIVE INCOME

Direct real estate deals are active rather than passive income investments, meaning you have to be involved somehow, whether it's management, accounting, or construction. That means you'll be spending more of your time working for your return. I don't care how good your property manager is, you *will* be taking calls to answer questions at some point. Even if you want someone to do the managing for you, you still have to find someone good enough and then manage them to make sure they're doing a good job. Even a great property manager doesn't control everything. In fact, you're doing all kinds of things if you're investing directly. One day you'll be out searching for a new home to buy. The next you'll be looking into rezoning a piece of property. The third you'll attend an inspection for a rental property, only to find out there is damage and you have to pay for the fixes. Other time is spent keeping track of who paid rent and sending a notice to those who didn't. If they get behind, there's an eviction process and a court process to get back rent. It can go on and on. Direct investing is not a good way to produce passive income.

Life is short. To me, time is far more valuable than money. I can always get more money, but I can't get more time. If you qualify to invest with someone like me, chances are you've already got something you're very good at that you spend your time doing. Why take on another job and headache when you can work with a sponsor who will take care of all the hard stuff? Why, in other words, would you not do the work once and get paid forever?

ASSESS YOUR SKILLS

If you do want to get your feet wet in direct real estate investing, as I did, you need to decide whether you'll be using a property to generate rental income or whether you want to fix and flip a property. Take an honest assessment of your skillset and see what you bring to the table. For example, an individual investor who has a lot of experience and knowledge in construction will likely know how to get building permits and assess what is and isn't up to code on a property. This information could put you at an advantage over someone who walks into a run-down home and has no idea how to fix it. Or maybe the only thing you bring to the table is money—there's value in that as well. Deal sponsors (like me) respect your money because we can't make a deal without it. If your greatest asset is money, then it might make less sense for you to fix and flip than it would for the construction guy.

When I was a real estate broker, I had all types of clients with different experience levels. One guy was basically a construction laborer. Instead of working for someone else for $30 an hour, he found totally destroyed houses and fixed them all by himself. By the time he turned around and sold them, he made closer to $100 an hour for his time. There are other people I worked with from an accounting background. These guys understood the tax advantages of investing in real estate, such as how to incorporate depreciation into their returns. Or I'd work with lawyers who understood contract law. My point is that most people have some type of skill they can bring to the table when investing in real estate; it's just a matter of defining what it is and letting that skill drive your choices.

GETTING STARTED IN DIRECT INVESTING

There are plenty of books on direct real estate investing. But this book isn't really about doing it yourself. It's about letting others do the work for you.

I'm sharing my knowledge and experience here, though, because by learning from me, you're already letting someone do the work for you. So I'll give you a crash course here in how to do it with the hope that you'll realize it's not worth it, while at the same time you'll see what the process is like, learning in a few minutes of reading what it took me years to understand.

When you first get started investing in real estate, start small just to learn how deals are done. Even if you're participating in a PPM, you don't necessarily need to put large chunks of money in a deal. Ask the sponsor if you can start with a small amount to see how the process works. Or let's say your income is $100,000 a year. You don't want to buy a million-dollar house to rent out, because if you don't have a tenant, you can't afford to pay the carry. So again, start small. Find a property small enough that you can handle a vacancy or a problem with the structure of the home. Likewise, you want to stay out of crime-ridden areas. Dealing with bad tenants and drug deals will be too challenging for a new investor—buy in a decent location.

Anyone can do this: you don't need to be accredited. You do, however, need to be very patient. Look at fifty properties (at least) before making a decision to buy one. It's like used car shopping: you go around to look at the different cars to make sure they work and you're getting a good price. If you want the best car for $8,000, you'll look at fifty or sixty cars to learn the market and know what you should be paying. The same applies to buying property. Once you look at enough deals, the good ones will stick out to you. If your patience causes you to miss a few deals along the way, no problem. As I always say, you make more money on the deals you don't do (say no to) than you do on the deals you do (say yes to).

Although you don't need to be accredited to make these direct real estate investments, do *not* borrow in order to get capital to invest. I have people ask me all the time if they should use their home equity line to make real estate deals. "I can borrow at 2 percent," they say. "Why don't I take that and make a 10 percent return?" I strongly advise people against doing this, as it goes against my philosophy. Your home and your IRA should be your ultimate safety net, so if anything goes wrong, you at least have a home you own free and clear at some point and an IRA as a backstop. You can borrow from a bank for *some* of the money to finance an investment. In fact, it's actually a good idea right now because the bank will be another set of eyes on the deal. (But beware, this can change. In 2002–2007 or so, banks would give you 100 percent of what you wanted to buy, and I'm not even sure they ever looked at anything.)

You may have a wealthy family or other resources that can help backstop you against financial ruin, but my advice to virtually everyone is that there's never a good, compelling reason to borrow off your home in order to invest in real estate or even consolidate debts. If you have credit card debt, pay it off. Don't put it on your house and pretend it's smart because you're paying a lower interest rate. (I know this isn't a financial book, but that's just my two cents on borrowing against your home.)

The bottom line: if you have enough money, you're going to want to stick 100 percent to passive investing and steer clear of direct investing. If you don't have enough money (yet!), you'll want to continue working to get some, or you might consider moonlighting in direct real estate investments.

But if passive investing is an option, then it's the only option. End of story.

REITS AND THEIR ADVANTAGES AND DISADVANTAGES

Another type of real estate investment opportunity is a REIT (real estate investment trust). As we touched on earlier, REITs are institutional-grade, publicly traded vehicles for investing in larger real estate deals. REITs typically focus on one asset class (e.g., manufactured home communities, apartments, industrial properties, office buildings, etc.). They own thousands of units and millions of square feet of whatever asset class they focus on, and anyone can participate. There's no need to be accredited because REITs are publicly traded on the stock market. As a result, they are a much more liquid form of real estate investment. You can trade in and out of the shares, but that acts as an advantage and a disadvantage.

CHANGING VALUES

The value of a REIT changes far faster than a private placement deal. For example, REITs have to pay out between 90 percent and 100 percent of their revenue to their shareholders. While it's designed to pay out money over time, because it's traded on the stock market and is so liquid, it ends up trading like bonds, where there is an inverse relationship between yield and price.

Here's what I mean by that: let's say you buy a REIT for $100 a share, and that share is yielding 3 percent in dividends, which works out to $0.75 per quarter. But if the United States experiences some inflation pressures and the Federal Reserve decides to raise interest rates, your bank might start paying you a decent interest rate on your savings account. There was a time when banks paid 6 percent on savings accounts. If we went back to that rate, suddenly the 3 percent yield on a REIT doesn't look as attractive. In short, with a REIT, the market can change so fast that it wipes out the yield you've been getting, virtually overnight.

THE ADVANTAGES AND DISADVANTAGES OF LIQUIDITY

Human behavior dictates that most people sell when they should buy and buy when they should sell. Take recessions, for example—when a recession happens, the overwhelming majority of people panic and proceed to liquidate whatever they can as asset values plummet. Some people, of course, have no choice. For those who do have a choice, the smart thing to actually do is not sell during a recession but in fact buy more assets. Think about it: if you had bought assets during the 2008 recession at depressed values, each dollar you invested would be worth significantly more in 2019, now that the economy has rebounded. The key is to stay patient and not panic. If you're one of the people who can ignore emotion and are able to stay disciplined with your investing, congrats! For you, the liquidity could be an advantage. For most people it is NOT an advantage.

In a private placement deal, you don't have a choice but to be patient. Your money is locked in, meaning you can't panic-sell when you see the price drop—you're forced to stay in for the long haul. If you have a good deal sponsor, you are likely to see the original return you were looking for. With REITs, if they drop, it takes time for the share price to recover. But there is an active market so you can sell when it's down, which is what most of us tend to do— it's human nature. It's another reason why PPMs with a solid sponsor are the way to go.

ANOTHER (BAD) KIND OF REIT

There are also non-traded private REITs. These are traded through a broker, who takes a huge commission on the transaction when you invest. This isn't beneficial if you're trying to make money. You're also beholden to a group of executives who run the company. There are typically many more fees and much more overhead associated with private REITs than a private placement memorandum. And because REITs typically work with much larger amounts of cash, they tend to miss out on the better prices of smaller properties. This is what creates the opportunities for PPM deals.

This, of course, isn't all or nothing. There might be some good private REITs, but it's tough to find an objective opinion about which ones make sense because the whole financial system is set up to "sell" them to you. When I have looked into these, I find most of my questions revolving around who wins and who loses in a venture. I've found that if the deal goes really well, the investors can do okay. Other than a very optimistic scenario, it's pretty bleak. So, could they work? Sure. Maybe. Who knows? But are they as safe as PPMs and do they have the same upside? In my opinion, no, but I work in the PPM space, so that's hardly an objective opinion.

So, let's talk about PPM deals.

PLACEMENT MEMORANDUMS: THE WAY TO GO

It's important to know how PPMs are structured. Although a PPM is a partnership that is filed under Form D with the Securities and Exchange Commission (SEC), it's generally a partnership that is free of cumbersome SEC filing expenses. When filing under Form D, a new PPM is created for every deal. A PPM is a document that lays out the specifics of how the deal works, projected benefits and risks, how the deal sponsor gets paid, and what management fees will be taken out. It's a very lengthy legal document. PPM deals are subject to some public reporting and oversight, but not very much. There's no institutional-grade scrutiny like you'd see on publicly traded investments. That (supposedly) is why there are laws in place to limit PPM deals to only accredited investors.

SMALL MEANS BIG

PPMs tend to be small, under-the-radar deals. You may come across a PPM for a large, very expensive project or acquisition, but for the most part, PPMs focus on raising $1 million to $20 million, as opposed to hundreds of millions for a REIT. One major advantage of a PPM deal is you can cut out all the conventional middlemen—brokers and advisors (and the fees that come with them). An Edward Jones advisor or your Charles Schwab guy isn't incentivized to get you to invest in PPMs. In fact, due to regulations, in most cases they CAN'T recommend them even if they wanted to.

Small can also be good for other reasons. It's easier to double your money on $10 than it is with $100 million. I could double $20,000 on real estate every year. I'd find an undervalued home that needs a little work, I'd put my $10,000 down, borrow $90,000 from the bank, fix it up with $10,000 more, then sell it for $130,000. I doubled my money. If you give me $100 million and ask me to do the same thing, it won't happen, or it will take a lot longer.

PPMs include existing properties and the development of new properties. Again, they're relatively illiquid, meaning they're buy-and-hold situations or build-and-sell situations (in other words, you can't just sell whenever you want as you could with, say, a stock). I think this is an advantage because you don't have someone on the street corner yelling what your price is every five minutes (metaphorically speaking). Your emotion is taken out of the equation—or at least, you can't act on your emotions. If you get scared about the deal and want to sell, you can't. You're forced to be patient. Some people are good at putting their money in an investment and then forgetting about it. I'm not like that. When I buy a stock, I look at it every day on my computer or phone and I get frustrated when it goes down, and it's never good enough when it goes up. It's essentially like gambling—and I stopped doing that a long time ago.

TAKE AWAY THE GAMBLE

I used to love gambling when I was younger—blackjack and craps, specifically. Once I got into the real world and earned an income, I'd go to Vegas with $2,000 and tell myself it was entertainment. If I *won* another $2,000, it wasn't lifechanging. It was nice but didn't feel like enough, and it just incentivized me to keep gambling and risk losing it all. If I lost the $2,000? All I could think about was what I could have done with that money—the things I could've bought, the vacations I could have gone on. That's how the stock market feels to me: the highs are never high enough, and the lows are too low. I love PPMs because they take away the feeling that I'm gambling.

If you are into gambling, then this book probably isn't for you. I'm the kind of guy who'd rather tip 35 percent and overpay babysitters than throw money at something, hope I get lucky, and then have more money. Investing, as I define it, means putting your money into something that will provide value. It's NOT about asking yourself, "How big can I make my stack?" If that all makes sense and you're nodding along with me, then get on as many potential investor lists as you can find and start reviewing deal decks and PPMs.

Yes, the risk-return equation applies to PPMs: more risk equals more potential return. However, I like to say that risk is proportionate to knowledge, meaning if you have no knowledge of the deal and aren't asking questions of your sponsor—and not reading this book—then you're being risky. But if you take a little more time and gain some knowledge about the person putting the deals together, then you'll have a higher chance of a good outcome. And if you're reading this book, then good, because vetting deal sponsors is what you're learning to do. And that's smart. It's not gambling.

BUILD YOUR CAKE AND EAT IT TOO

The illiquid nature of PPMs means you don't want to put the bulk of your assets in private placements, because then you'll have no access to your capital. Instead, map out when you'll need access to your money. I look at it like a wedding cake. The bottom layer is the last chunk of money I'll need to get to. That bottom layer (the largest) is where I'll invest in illiquid assets like PPMs. The middle layer is where I'll keep stocks, which I may want to sell at an opportune time. The top layer is cash. You should keep a top layer of 20 percent cash at all times. If there's a dip in the market and you want to buy more stocks, you have the ability to do so with cash on hand.

You can also have cash around to further build that bottom

layer of the cake. Good PPM deals are the hidden gems of investing, but you need the cash available to invest in them. Finding good PPM deals takes time and energy. It also takes experience. Find somebody who has twenty to twenty-five years of learning and mastering the craft of finding PPM deals. You can look at it two ways: either you can be the one reading every private placement memorandum that you can get your hands on, or you can find somebody who is very good at it already. I suggest you do the latter. HINT: this is what the wealthiest, smartest investors do. It's also what you're learning to do in this book.

PPM CASE STUDIES

A good private placement deal will sometimes look very boring on the surface. This is typically a good thing. Remember, the sexier the PPM deal, the worse the return (typically). The best PPMs have taken some kind of problem or challenge and provided a solution. Straight talk is what you are looking for—something that is easy to understand.

TRASH MAKES CASH

An example is a situation we just refer to as Trolley Industrial Drive. It is a 240,000-square-foot industrial building that had about 80,000 square feet built over an unregulated landfill. The floors started collapsing over the landfill, and the owner of the building blamed the tenant, saying that they caused the floors to collapse and they had to fix it. The tenant, however, bored through the floors and found the truth: the building was built on an unregulated and unrecorded landfill that no one knew about. The tenant told the owner that methane gas had built up and they were leaving the building. That portion of the building was now vacant, meaning there was no income. The owner tried to give the building back to the bank, but the bank didn't want it—even banks want nothing to do with environmental problems. We came in, bought the loan from the bank for $1.2 million, and immediately obtained clear title to the property with all cash. We estimated it would cost another $1.2 million to rip out the 80,000 square feet on the landfill and put in a methane mitigation system that would vent any gases out of the building. Within one year, we had all the repairs done. The $2.7 million we put into it (we went over budget on the repairs) worked out to about $11 per square foot. Now it rents for about $4 a square foot. That's $960,000 a year on a $2.7 million investment.

We recently put a $6 million loan on that building. This means we got all of our initial investment back, plus a big pile of cash. None of that is taxable either, because the money came out as proceeds from a loan. Was it a sexy deal? Certainly not, but it made money.

KNOWLEDGE IS POWER...OR AT LEAST MONEY

Deals like these don't grow on trees. They're situations we could capitalize on because we understood the issues at play and have the experience to pull it off. They were home run deals. In addition, they created value for people—not just the investors.

These situations happen all the time. The key is having someone with the experience and expertise to find the deal, structure it, AND SEE IT THROUGH. That's what you are looking for: someone who does this for a living and needs YOU because they don't have all the money themselves. How do you find these people? PROSPECT-ING! (See Chapter Two).

Conclusion

As I said in the introduction, this book is for professionals and business owners who have limited time and energy to nitpick the details of real estate investment deals. It's for people who have money to invest in real estate but need a good steward for that money—somebody who will take care of it. I hope a few younger deal sponsors out there find it useful as well.

How can you find more information about real estate PPMs? Other than this book, if you're interested in information about PPMs and real estate investing in general, you can start by simply Googling "private placement memorandums." Read a few of them and get in contact with the people putting them together. Ask around to your friends and colleagues to see if they know of good people. Believe me: real estate investing is a much smaller world than you'd think. Call people up. Have conversations with them to learn more about investing. Everyone is busy, I get that, but you need to set some time aside to sit down and look at these PPM deals and have those conversations. In reality, it doesn't take that long to do a couple of Google searches, pick up the phone, and ask a few questions. Also, keep educating yourself. Samuel K. Freshman's *Principles of Real Estate Syndication* is a great book to reference. It lays out exactly how to do what I do and even further familiarizes you with the process. Podcasts are another great resource for learning about real estate AND for finding sponsors who are looking for investors. Your time is finite, and that's why you need a deal sponsor you can trust and work with, for as long as it makes sense. Tell yourself to work hard once (finding someone you can invest with) and then get paid forever. After that, please enjoy, live, do things, spend, help people—money by itself is worthless, unless you have really low self-esteem and use it as a measuring stick.

If you're interested in learning more about how these deals are made, you can easily get your hands on, say, ten PPMs from different deal sponsors and gain a whole lot of insight into real estate and business in general. PPMs are relatively easy to understand—they're mostly written in plain English. The point is that most people will be more than willing to share this information with you because informed investors are smart and patient investors, and that makes everyone's life easier. The deal sponsor should be able to explain their investments to you in terms you can understand. If they can't do that, then don't invest with them.

HOW CAN WE HELP?

We will gladly put anyone on our investor list and share any and all information we have about our deals. We'll send you what we send to our investors so you can have benchmarks for our different deals and see what works and what doesn't. Again, I suggest you interview more than one sponsor. If you're running into roadblocks getting information on a private placement memorandum, shoot us an email at ir@promanas.com.

It's a lot easier to contact us, ask us questions, and get referrals from us than it is to figure out the nitty-gritty of a PPM on your own. I would never begrudge anyone from learning, and I stand by the advice that you should learn a bit about PPMs, but the whole point of this book is to tell you how to find a partner who can take care of the details for you. Do the work to find that right partner one time, and you'll get paid forever.